Fifth Edition

SENCos have a key role to play in developing and implementing an inclusive framework for meeting Special Educational Needs

The fifth edition of this best-selling *SENCo Handbook* provides up-to-date information and advice in relation to three key government publications: *Removing Barriers to Achievement: The Government's Strategy for SEN* (2004), *Every Child Matters: Change for Children in Schools* (2004) and the Disability Discrimination Act (2005), particularly the disability equality duty and accessibility plan.

Elizabeth Cowne offers clear and practical guidance to SENCos enabling them to meet the demands made on them by the latest legislation and practice. This comprehensive companion:

- Introduces the reader to the key concepts and issues of SEN and inclusion
- Provides detailed information for SENCos, head teachers and governors about developing whole-school policy and practice for children and young people with SEN
- Advises on essential aspects of the role of SENCos' including the management of support staff, working in partnership with parents and outside agencies and the improvement of teaching and learning
- Enables those working in education to debate, discuss and reflect on the issues presented in relation to their work in schools or other settings
- Includes a photocopiable section of staff development activities
- Gives information on further reading and source materials.

The SENCo Handbook remains essential reading for all those responsible for special educational needs working in early years, primary, secondary and FE settings.

Elizabeth Cowne tutors on the Education Doctorate programme in the Open University and has been actively involved in the professional development of SENCos since 1983.

KEY TEXT REFERENCE

THE SENCo HANDBOOK

Working within a Whole-School Approach

FIFTH EDITION

Elizabeth Cowne

Routledge
Taylor & Francis Group

LONDON AND NEW YORK

Fifth edition published 2008
by Routledge
2 Park Square, Milton Park, Abingdon, Oxon, OX14 4RN

Simultaneously published in the USA and Canada
by Routledge
270 Madison Avenue, New York, NY 10016

First published 1996 by David Fulton Publishers
Second edition 1998
Third edition 2000
Fourth edition 2003

Routledge is an imprint of the Taylor & Francis Group, an informa business

Typeset in Garamond by
RefineCatch Ltd, Bungay, Suffolk
Printed and bound in Great Britain by
Bell & Bain, Glasgow

British Library Cataloguing in Publication Data
A catalogue record for this book is available from the British Library

Library of Congress Cataloging in Publication Data
The SENCo handbook: working within a whole school approach/Elizabeth Cowne.
– 5th ed.
    p. cm.
Includes bibliographical references and index.
1. Special education–Great Britain–Administration–Handbooks, manuals, etc.
LC3986.G7C69 2008
371.9′04–dc22

                                                                    2008003333

ISBN13: 978-0-415-45367-7 (pbk)
ISBN10: 0-415-45367-4 (pbk)

Contents

Foreword

The author of a book supporting the work of SENCos must have great practical expertise and understanding of schools, a commitment to achieving the best for all pupils and the ability to take a broad view, both in relation to historical developments and national, local and individual school systems. Liz Cowne meets all the criteria. She has a long background in mainstream school work with SEN, and has been involved since 1983 in innovative teacher training for SENCos at the Institute of Education, University of London.

Increasingly the SENCo is accepted as a key member of the senior leadership team. She is a manager, a developer of staff expertise, an evaluator of group and individual progress and, above all, an agent of change. The book explores all these areas and presents well-tested models of management and staff development for readers to bring into their practice.

Liz Cowne's ability to provide a theoretical context to practical ideas is shown at its best in her discussion of the Individual Education Plan and alternatives like provision mapping, in relation to curriculum design. The whole book gives a welcome emphasis to the SENCo's role in relation to curriculum development, which can easily be neglected in the pressures of other aspects of the job.

Three close colleagues, Pam Wright, Liz Gerschel and Carol Frankl, have helped Liz Cowne revise this book. They have contributed their considerable knowledge and experience gained through teaching the Institute of Education's Outreach SENCo training courses for the last eight years.

Liz and her colleagues have renewed a resource which addresses all the demands of developing practice and recent legislation and guidance, including the Disability Discrimination Acts and *Every Child Matters*. It will be invaluable to all SENCos and those who work with them and train them.

Nick Peacey, Coordinator, SENJIT,
Institute of Education, University of London
November 2007

Acknowledgements

The author would like to thank the many colleagues who have contributed inspiration to, or advice on, the writing of this book. I owe the original idea for the book to Judith Jones who edited and all the colleagues in the Learning Support Group and Merton schools who contributed to the Merton version of a *SENCo Handbook*, produced for their schools.

I also owe a debt to the hundreds of course members from all phases of education, and from most LAs in the Greater London area, with whom I have worked since 1983. Their projects, on curriculum differentiation and other aspects of whole-school policy development, carried out as part of Special Educational Needs in Ordinary Schools (SENIOS) and more recently from the SENCo training modules run from the Institute of Education, have given me in-depth knowledge of how SENCos manage change. From small beginnings and working within many constraints, these teachers and thousands like them have developed the good practice which benefits children with special educational needs in mainstream schools, much of which is now embodied in the National Standards for SEN Coordination (Teacher Training Agency: TTA 1998).

For this edition, I am much indebted to Carol Frankl, Liz Gerschel and Pam Wright (Newham) who have edited and contributed to all the present chapters and activities, and without whose help, this edition would not have been possible.

I would also like to thank the following individuals for their constructive criticism and advice about the chapters they read in draft: Christine Clatworthy, Christine Duckworth, Linda Roberts (members of the Merton Learning Support Services), Bernie Marcou (Merton SENCo). Also, Paul Greenhalgh, Mary Hrekow, Sabina Melidi, Susan Murray, Nick Peacey and Judith Wade who helped with additional information and advice for the original edition. My thanks also to Zoe Brown, Colin Hardy, Ruth MacConville, Ann-Marie McNicholas, Mike Murphy, Anne Rawlings and Jim Wight for additional advice for later editions.

My thanks goes most to my daughter Alison, for her hard work, patience and skill in producing the typed copy and for making the production of the book possible. Crown copyright is reproduced with the permission of the Controller of HMSO.

Elizabeth Cowne 2008

How to use this Handbook

This book is intended to help SENCos, head teachers and governors to implement an effective policy and practice for special educational needs in every school. The following guidance notes on each chapter are to tell you how to find what you need and to link the themes which run through the chapters. The book begins with a debate on issues about SEN and their historic and legislative origins. This could be useful if you wish to get your staff to look at their concepts of special needs and the value systems of the school. Other staff development activities are to be found in the Activity Pack at the back of the book.

Chapter 1: Decisions and Dilemmas in SEN: Legislative and Historical Perspectives

The purpose of this chapter is to outline the history of special educational needs legislation and practice, in order to examine changing perspectives and attitudes left as a legacy from the past. Important new government documents have been issued which are briefly described in the revised chapter. These include: Every Child Matters: Change for Children (2004); Children Act (2004); Removing Barriers to Achievement: The Government's strategy for SEN (2004); and The Duty to Promote Disability Equality: Statutory Code of Practice (TSO 2005).

Chapter 2: Roles and Responsibilities within Whole-school SEN Coordination

This chapter begins by outlining the roles of governors, head, SENCo and class teachers as described in the Code of Practice (DfES 2001b) and the Disability Rights Commission Code of Practice (2002a; 2002b). The chapter continues by discussing the SENCo's role in leading and managing others. Activities 1 and 2 support this section. The chapter ends by considering how to monitor and evaluate the effectiveness of whole-school policies for SEN. Activity 6 can be used in conjunction with this topic. Themes continue in Chapters 6 and 9.

Chapter 3: Identification, Assessment and Planning for Progress

This chapter examines in turn, issues of identification, types of assessment and the links between assessment and planning for pupils with a range of learning difficulties and disabilities (LDD). IEPs and the use of alternatives are discussed including Provision Mapping. The chapter ends with a discussion of the SENCo role in decision-making in relation to the graduated response of the Code of Practice (DfES 2001b). Activity 4 links with this chapter.

Chapter 4: *The Curriculum: Planning for an Inclusive Curriculum*

Three perspectives on differentiation are considered: behavioural, cognitive and one which considers the affective domain. The implications of these perspectives are put into the framework of whole-school curriculum planning.

Chapter 5: *The Curriculum: Key Issues for Key Stages*

This second chapter on the curriculum gives practical ideas for SENCos to work with colleagues on differentiation in each of the National Curriculum Key Stages and in FE. Activity 3 is a staff development exercise on lesson planning in any of Key Stages 1 to 3.

Chapter 6: *Managing Effective Support*

This chapter covers aspects of the SENCo's role in providing and managing the schools' support policy and practice. Types of support are described, as is the role of the teaching assistant (TA). The importance of liaison time for support staff and good quality training is emphasised. Next, is a section on support for, and training of SENCos. There is additional guidance on reviewing support policies. Activity 5 links to this review process.

Chapter 7: *Multi-professional Networks*

This chapter looks at one of the key roles of SENCos: to build relationships with outside services and agencies, other schools and the networks of voluntary organisations. Source List 2 contains useful addresses of voluntary organisations.

Chapter 8: *Working in Partnership at Transition Periods*

Partnership with other professionals at critical transition points in the pupils' careers is also described: entry to school, phase transfer, and transition planning at 13+, including transition to further education.

Chapter 9: *Managing Paperwork and Procedures: the Coordinating Role*

The bureaucratic role of the SENCo is discussed, including running annual reviews for those with statements. Other quasi-legal aspects, such as the Special Educational Needs and Disability Tribunal (SENDIST) and Ofsted inspections are covered. It should be read in conjunction with Chapter 3.

Chapter 10: *Working with People: the Consultative Role*

This chapter considers the consultative aspect of the SENCo's role; working with children, parents, teachers and governors and makes links to the roles discussed in other chapters. Appendix 10 contains notes on observation methods and other ideas for understanding the pupil's perspective.

Chapter 11: *Working Together towards Inclusive Practice*

This chapter examines the changing concept of inclusion and how this relates to the SENCo's role. The chapter ends by showing how this book can support SENCos' reflective thinking and their role as an agent of change.

Abbreviations

AfL	Assessment for Learning
ASDAN	Award Scheme Development Accreditation Network
AWPU	Age/Weighted Pupil Unit
BESD	Behavioural, Emotional and Social Difficulties
BEST	Behaviour and Education Support Team
CAF	Common Assessment Framework
CAMHS	Child and Adolescent Mental Health Services
CASE	Cognitive Acceleration through Science
CIS	Children's Information Services
COP	Code of Practice
CPD	Continuing Professional Development
DCSF	Department for Children, Schools and Families
DDA	Disability Discrimination Act
DES	Department of Education and Schools
DfEE	Department for Education and Employment
DfES	Department for Education and Schools
DoH	Department of Health
DRC	Disability Rights Commission
EAL	English as an Additional Language
ECM	Every Child Matters
EMA	Ethnic Minority Achievement
EP	Education Psychologist
EPS	Educational Psychological Service
EWO	Education Welfare Officer
EWS	Educational Welfare Service
EYDCP	Early Years Development and Child Care Partnership
FE	Further Education
FEFC	Further Education and Funding Council
GCSE	General Certificate in Secondary Education
GEP	Group Education Plan
GNVQ	General National Vocational Qualification
HLTA	Higher Level Teaching Assistant
ICT	Information Communication technology
IEP	Individual Education Plan
IHE	Institutes of Higher Education
JCQ	Joint Council for Qualifications
KS	Key Stage
LDD	Learning Difficulties and Disabilities
LA	Local Authority

LEA	Local Education Authority
LMS	Local Management of Schools
LSA	Learning Support Assistant
LSC	Learning and Skills Council
NASEN	National Association of Special Educational Needs
NUT	National Union of Teachers
NVQ	National Vocational Qualification
Ofsted	Office for Standards in Education
PLASC	Pupil Level Annual School Census
PRU	Pupil Referral Unit
PSHE	Personal and Social Health Education
PSP	Pastoral Support Programme
QCA	Qualifications and Curriculum Authority
SAT	Standard Assessment Test
SEAL	Social and Emotional Aspects of Learning
SEF	Self Evaluation Form
SEN	Special Educational Needs
SENCo	Special Educational Needs coordinator
SENDA	Special Educational Needs and Disability Act
SENDIST	Special Educational Needs and Disability Tribunal
SENIOS	Special Educational Needs in Ordinary Schools
SENJIT	Special Educational Needs Joint Initiative for Training
SENSSA	Special Educational Needs Support Services Association (www.senssa.co.uk)
SIP	School's Improvement Plan
SLT	Senior Leadership Team
TA	Teaching Assistant
TDA	Teacher Development Agency
TSO	The Stationery Office
VAK	Visual, Auditory, Kinaesthetic

CHAPTER 1

Decisions and Dilemmas in Special Educational Needs

Legislative and Historical Perspectives

This chapter begins by exploring some of the historical background of special education in England and Wales and examines changes in attitudes and terminology towards children with a range of disabilities and learning difficulties.

The first hundred years of compulsory schooling began in 1870 with the Elementary Education Act. In the decades which followed, pressure grew from school boards and voluntary groups to provide a separate system for educating pupils with disabilities. Children with disabilities were seen as unfit for the large classes of fifty or more taught by teachers with no specialist training. The usual solution was to segregate these children into a special school. Funds to run these often came from charities. By 1918 some school boards in metropolitan areas were educating the 'unfit' in special classes within normal schools. Others with disabilities were provided for by a mixture of institutions or by home visiting. The voluntary charitable societies developed a professional expertise in offering vocational training as well as care for particular groups, such as the blind and the deaf.

Special education had higher costs, so only some school boards offered provision in classes or special schools. Rural communities often kept their disabled pupils within their normal schools or gave no schooling at all. Universal access to education for all children with disabilities was to come later. This segregation and isolation often meant that disabled children were denied access to the normal activities and opportunities of the local school and community. In some cases where the disabled child did attend a village school their needs may not have been understood and they often suffered ridicule.

The 1944 Act

At the end of the Second World War, the 1944 Act was passed. The policy behind this Act was to provide statutory education at primary and secondary stages to all children, including those with disabilities. The only exceptions were those who had a severe mental handicap, for whom it took a further 26 years and new legislation to give Education Authorities the responsibility for their education. The 1944 Act stated that:

> Local Educational Authorities should secure that provision is made for pupils who suffer from any disability of mind or body, by providing either in special schools or otherwise, special educational treatment, that is to say education by special methods for persons suffering from that disability.

(see Appendix 1a, categories from 1959)

The LEA was to ascertain which children needed special treatment and then decide on placement according to category. The advice used to make this decision came largely from medical officers. Later, psychologists began to be employed to test this group of children and to assist the medical officers in their decision-making. As Tomlinson remarks:

> The history of special education must be viewed in terms of the benefits it brought for a developing industrial society, the benefits for the normal mass education system of a special sub-system of education and the benefits that medical, psychological, educational personnel derive from encouraging new areas of professional expertise.
>
> (Tomlinson 1982)

Towards the end of the period 1944–78 much had changed. A complex special education system of schools, classes and services had been built up. Teacher training in SEN specialisms had developed. Children with severe learning difficulties were at last given the right to education through the Handicapped Children Act (1970). Parents had begun, through voluntary groups, to exert pressure for change. Influences from abroad (the USA in particular) were affecting the thinking of such groups. The Warnock Committee, set up in 1974, produced a report in 1978. From this grew the most significant legislation for special education – the 1981 Act.

The 1981 Act

The 1981 Act redefined the population of pupils with disabilities as those with 'special educational needs'. This Act gave clear guidelines about assessment procedures and the issuing of a statement of special educational needs. Statements are documents which summarise a pupil's learning difficulties and list suitable provision. Building on the recommendations of the Warnock report much was said in the 1981 Act about involving parents in decision-making in relation to assessment. Schools were also given responsibilities to identify the full range of those with SEN using the five-stage assessment procedure suggested in the Warnock report.

The term 'special educational needs' depends not only on a concept of discontinuity of provision, but also on the concept of relativity of need. This is the most fundamental dilemma of special educational needs, because although the term includes children with disabilities, it also includes those whose educational progress in learning is significantly slower than that of their peer group, for whatever cause. To identify which individuals have such needs and so require something extra or something different from what is normally provided requires a decision-making process.

The 1981 Act embodied much of what had been developing over time and could be perceived as building on 'best practice'. The 1981 Act influenced attitudes of teachers in mainstream schools. Some began to recognise that pupils with SEN were their responsibility. Integration policies were adopted by many schools and LEAs. Training for special educational needs in ordinary schools (SENIOS) was funded through training grants from 1983 onwards (DES Circulars 3/83–85). Those responsible for special needs provision in schools were not, at this time, called special educational needs coordinators. This responsibility was often taken by either a member of the senior management team or was in the hands of the 'remedial' teacher or team.

Between 1983 and 1994 the role of the SENCo became fully established and a description of the role was written into the Code of Practice (1994). In 1998 the Teacher Training Agency (TTA) published the *National Standards for Special Educational Needs Coordinators*. These set out the core purposes of the role of the SENCo and the key outcomes of SEN coordination. These standards enhance the role of the SENCo, bringing it into higher profile. They were also being used as guidelines for SENCo training courses.

Multi-professional decision-making

The more complex a child's need, the more people will be involved in the decision-making process within and across organisations and professions. Communication between these individuals and organisations is important if coherent and consistent decisions are to be made. The power base of those who make such decisions has changed across the century. In the earliest decades, the medical profession, often alone, chose which child went to a special school or indeed had any schooling at all. The LEA was expected to ascertain which children needed special treatment and decide on placement according to category, but the advice used to make this decision came largely from medical officers (see Appendix 1a). Sutton (1982) states that:

> For years, it remained unclear who were the gate keepers to special education and despite the law's clear statement that the final decision lay with the LEA, in practice the actual decision very often lay with a medical officer following prescribed procedures.
>
> (Sutton 1982: 11)

The 1981 Act attached great value to multi-disciplinary assessment. The power of the medical profession and its model, which had affected special education for so long, was reduced. The focus was on educational needs and these were to be described in educational terms and met by educational provision. Treatment was not a word used in describing this provision. Guidance on assessment and statements was given through Circular 1/83.

The 1981 Act required joint decision-making between health, education and social services. Parents began to have some say in their child's assessment and voluntary organisations began to lobby on behalf of different groups of children.

Provision was made across what Fish (1989) called dimensions of need, all of which lie on a continuum. Decision-making becomes complex when the providers of various resources have different priorities. Education, for example, may specify that health authorities should provide therapies for children with SEN, but the health authority may not see this as a priority area for their resources. This is a further dilemma which arises between cross-professional provision: one which must be resolved on a regional or national level.

The Education Reform Act (1988)

The Education Reform Act (1988) contributed to the thinking of a new perspective on pupils with learning difficulties. This Act stated that all children have a right to a 'broad, balanced, relevant and differentiated curriculum'. On the positive side this meant all pupils now had an 'entitlement curriculum'. On the negative side teachers were overloaded by the requirement to teach the number of subjects specified and to test and assess pupils' progress in all of these subjects. Schools began to be more aware of their overall performance as judged by these tests. Pupils with special educational needs were not always seen as an asset when comparative tables of results were produced. This Act also introduced Local Management of Schools (LMS) and from then onwards schools required responsibility for most aspects of funding, including the provision for children with SEN.

The Children Act (1989)

This Act, though not focused on education, was influential in changing viewpoints about children's rights and parental responsibilities. It also influenced thinking about these rights within the Education Act (1993) and the Code of Practice (1994). The Code of Practice (2001) has a whole chapter on pupil participation. This chapter states very clearly that all children and young people have rights. This includes being involved in making decisions and exercising choices.

The 1993 Act and Code of Practice (1994)

The Education Act (1993) (Part 3) replaced much of the 1981 legislation without significant changes. The new elements were the setting up of the SEN tribunal and the publishing of the *Code of Practice on the Identification and Assessment of Special*

Educational Needs. This document has a status between a regulation, which is mandatory, and a circular which is advisory. Schools and LEAs are required to use their best endeavours to 'have regard to' the requirements of the Code of Practice to make provision for pupils with SEN. However, certain parts are mandatory.

The Act (1993) and Code of Practice (1994) pushed the decision-making surrounding statement and provision further towards schools and parents, but final decisions were still made by the LEAs, who took advice from other professionals through the multi-disciplinary assessment. Parents can and do initiate requests for assessment and have an increasing amount of power when exercised through the SEN tribunal. The number of cases going to tribunal has risen continually since it was set up, although there is concern that litigation is not the most effective or efficient way to resolve disputes. The 1996 Act replaced that of 1993, consolidating various pieces of legislation, but not making major changes in relation to SEN. This Act did state that schools must identify, assess and make provision for pupils with SEN. It also said that LEAs must provide maintained schools with auxiliary aids, such as laptop computers or braillers, and transport where needed.

National Curriculum revisions

In 1994 the Dearing Revision of the National Curriculum was issued. This was an attempt to 'slim down' the original orders and to 'lighten the load' for teachers. Guidance documents were issued which gave schools more flexibility in planning the curriculum and suggested that the school's population be considered in some detail when planning schemes of work. Special arrangements were put in place to vary assessments for pupils with statements.

But during the same period, secondary schools were required to publish their exam results and these could be compared through league tables in the local and national press. League tables are now also published for KS2 and KS3 English, Mathematics and Science. In 1998 the National Frameworks for Literacy and Numeracy were drawn up and these strategies are now in place in all primary schools – now also extended to KS3. However, these initiatives did not always give sufficient attention to the needs of those with disabilities or learning difficulties.

The National Curriculum was revised again at the end of 1999. The intention was that the need to disapply the National Curriculum for certain pupils should be kept to a minimum. The document explains in detail how principles of inclusion can be put into practice. The Inclusion Statement reminds us that schools have the responsibility of providing a broad and balanced curriculum for all pupils.

> This statutory inclusion statement on providing effective learning opportunities for all pupils outlines how teachers can modify, as necessary, the National Curriculum programmes of study to provide all pupils with relevant and appropriately challenging work at each key stage. It sets out three principles that are essential to developing a more inclusive curriculum:
> A. Setting suitable learning challenges
> B. Responding to pupils' diverse learning needs
> C. Overcoming potential barriers to learning and assessment for individuals and groups of pupils.
>
> Applying these principles should keep to a minimum the need for aspects of the National Curriculum to be disapplied for a pupil. Schools are able to provide other curricular opportunities outside the National Curriculum to meet the needs of individuals or groups of pupils such as speech and language therapy and mobility training.
> (DfES/QCA 1999, www.nc.uk.net/nc-resources/html/inclusion.stmii)

SEN Code of Practice (2001)

The Code of Practice (DfES 2001b) is differently structured to make it more accessible to readers. It also included new chapters which emphasise the importance of working in partnership with parents and listening to pupils' views. SEN categories were reintroduced (see Appendix 1b).

The sections on Identification and Assessment are presented for three phases: early education settings, primary and secondary phases. The staged assessment procedure is simplified and revised into a graduated response. The school based stages were to be called *School Action* and *School Action Plus*. Interventions should be recorded on IEPs for pupils at these stages and for those statements of SEN. The last chapter of the Code of Practice (DfES 2001b) describes the working partnership between agencies. The *SEN Toolkit* (DfES 2001c) was published at the same time as the Code to give practical advice.

Disability Discrimination Act (1995)

The poverty, disadvantage and social exclusion experienced by many disabled people is not the inevitable result of their impairments or medical conditions, but rather stems from attitudinal and environmental barriers. This is known as the 'social model of disability', and provides a basis for the successful implementation of the duty to promote disability equality. (TSO 2005: Appendix E, 172)

The Disability Discrimination Act (1995) (DDA) became law some twenty years after similar attempts to outlaw sex (1975) and race discrimination (1976) became statutory. Part 4 of the DDA (1995) applied to schools and introduced some employment rights for staff with disabilities; the requirement for schools to increase access to the curriculum, environment and information; and banned overt discrimination on the grounds of disability which limited access to the school's facilities and services. Overall however, its impact on schools was limited (see Appendix 1c, Definition of disability).

The Special Educational Needs and Disability Act (2001)

This Act known as SENDA, amended part 4 of the DDA (1995) and introduced the obligation upon schools to publish an Accessibility Plan, showing how access would be improved, over a three-year period, to the curriculum, the environment and to information, for pupils with learning difficulties and disabilities. This means that school planning and policies should address three distinct elements:

- improvements in access to the curriculum;
- physical improvements to increase access to education and associated services;
- improvements in the provision of information in a range of formats for disabled pupils.

This duty is proactive: schools may no longer wait for pupils with disabilities and learning difficulties to arrive, but must plan ahead in the expectation that such children will be part of their regular intake. Schools must not discriminate, nor give less favourable treatment to pupils with disabilities and learning difficulties on the grounds of their disability. In order to ensure equality, schools are expected to make reasonable adjustments to their provision so as to provide the increased access required. Excellent guidance on the duties of schools is offered in the Disability Code of Practice (TSO 2002) and the issue of what is a reasonable adjustment has been clarified by practice and by SEN and Disability Tribunals. This guidance also prepared the way for later amendments to the DDA (1995) in 2005, in particular, the Disability Equality Duty.

Every Child Matters: Change for Children (2004)

Every Child Matters: Change for Children [ECM] (DfES 2004a) is the Government's vision for a radical reshaping in children's services and improvements in opportunities and outcomes for all children and young people from birth to 19.

It aims to resolve some of the problems of multi-agency working to facilitate better information sharing. The key objective is intervention as early as possible to ensure the education and well-being of the whole child and prevent some children 'slipping through the net'.

The rationale of ECM is that pupil performance and wellbeing are interlinked. Its purpose is to base the changes on the five key aspects that children and young people need:

- being healthy
- staying safe
- enjoying and achieving
- making a positive contribution
- achieving economic well-being

Ofsted and other inspectorates judge the contribution of all the services to improving outcomes in each of these areas, including observing what action is being taken to ensure that 'children with learning difficulties and disabilities are helped' towards each of the outcomes.

The Children Act (2004)

The Children Act (2004) provides the legal framework for the programme of reform. Under this Act all local authorities in England were required to appoint a Director of Children's Services by 2008. Children's Trusts will be set up by April 2008 to unite Health, Education and Social Services and will work with all local partnerships, including voluntary organisations. LAs are required to set up databases of all children in their area, the services each child is known to, and the contact details of the relevant professionals who work with them.

Although the reform of children's services applies to the welfare of all children, the focus is on those children who are considered the most vulnerable and at risk of poor outcomes, including:

- children looked after
- children with mental health issues
- children with disabilities and complex needs

SENCos must be aware of how meeting the needs of children with SEN fits into the overall framework and must develop the skills which will be required to fulfill their changing role, for example, in the areas of:

- leading, managing and training staff
- challenging, coaching and advising
- managing and procuring resources
- strategic SEN improvement planning
- developing whole-school inclusive practice
- being the 'lead professional'.

Schools work towards the ECM outcomes through common processes, including the Common Assessment Framework (CAF). This is a process (using a checklist) to help practitioners, from a range of local authority and voluntary services, obtain a complete picture of a child's additional needs at an early stage. Its purpose is to enable better-targeted referrals to specialist services and to ensure that basic information follows the child to reduce duplication and increase safety. Its watch words are swift and easy access, early identification and prevention. The CAF must be in operation nationally by April 2008.

Children who need the support of several specialist agencies must have a lead professional to coordinate services for them. This person will be the single point of contact for families; the SENCo may very well take on this role or, at least, will be the school link, or named individual. SENCos, along with other school staff, will need to collaborate with other practitioners such as social workers, nurses, general practitioners and educational psychologists, which may involve joint training or working, or encouraging others to support what the school is doing in specific areas.

Alongside these changes, by 2010 all children should have access to a variety of activities beyond the school day, and a range of additional services. These extended services will both benefit pupils and help to build stronger relationships with parents and the wider community. These services may be on or off the school site but any services that a school develops must be available to the whole pupil population. This may present challenges to the SENCo when advising on arrangements for appropriate activities and ensuring that they and information about them are accessible to all families.

Removing Barriers to Achievement (2004)

The government's strategy for achieving their vision to enable pupils with special needs and disabilities to succeed is set out in the document *Removing Barriers to Achievement*. The four key areas are:

- early intervention
- removing barriers to learning
- raising expectation and achievement
- delivering improvements in partnership.

This strategy is born out of the Every Child Matters agenda and aims to ensure children have a good education and have regular opportunities to play within their local community. Increasing parental confidence that their children's needs will be met should reduce requests for statementing. The creation of children's trusts to integrate health, social care and education services to children and families is seen as essential to ensure seamless provision for vulnerable children. The CAF will be a key tool in promoting the integration of services; however, it will not replace the statutory process of statementing. Raising expectations and achievement for SEN pupils will focus on personalised learning and on the impact of interventions on pupil learning. Training for staff to improve understanding of SEN issues and how to tackle them effectively is being delivered through the National Strategy and is strengthened by the recommendations of the Select Committee for Education and Skills (2006) which recommends mandatory training for all new SENCos.

Disability Equality Duty Scheme (2006)

Overall, SENDA (2001) had significant impact on mainstream schools, in overcoming the barriers to inclusion; nevertheless, barriers remain.

> Although these barriers may be unintentional, that does not make their impact upon disabled people any less significant. When buildings, services and employment practices are designed in a way that fails to take into account the particular circumstances of disabled people, this excludes and disadvantages them. The same applies when budgets are set for a programme without adequately considering the additional needs of disabled people.
>
> (TSO 2005: 1.8)

It is perhaps the definition of disability that is having far-reaching and inclusive effects. It means that all people (children and adults) with learning difficulties are protected by the law from discrimination and also all those with disabilities and sensory impairments, mental health problems or diagnosed long-term illnesses such as cancer, even if these do not impair their learning or work.

> A person has a disability if he or she has a physical or mental impairment, which has a substantial and long-term adverse effect on his or her ability to carry out normal

day-to-day activities. Impairment can be physical or mental. This includes sensory impairments, such as those affecting sight or hearing. The term 'mental impairment' is intended to cover a wide range of impairments relating to mental functioning, including what are often known as learning disabilities.

(*The Duty to Promote Disability Equality: Statutory Code of Practice*, TSO 2005: Appendix B)

It is a measure of the strength of this legislation, with its focus on presence, participation and achievement, and its structures for implementation and change, that the format has been adopted by the Equal Opportunities Commission and government to introduce a similar Gender Equality Duty (2007). More details about implementation of the scheme are to be found in Chapter 2.

Dilemmas about Resourcing

Extra resourcing for special educational needs makes assumptions about what constitutes normal provision across schools or local authorities. Although schools are required to allocate funds between and amongst their pupils with special educational needs in an equitable manner, schools differ in the amount they allocate to their special educational needs budget. LAs also differ in the amount of additional funding they devolve to their schools.

At the time of the 1981 Act, Statements were seen as being for those children with quite exceptional and complex needs, but over the next decade or two, the trend was to increase the number of requests for assessments. The process of issuing statements is costly, so although the outcome is usually valued by parents, LAs now try to limit the number of multi-professional assessments to those they consider are in greatest need, especially as most funding is devolved to schools.

Government policy on inclusion has encouraged schools so accept the majority of children with disabilities and learning difficulties into mainstream provision. Devolved funding gives schools the full responsibility to organise and resource suitable provision for this wider range of pupils, which might include 'low impact–high incidence' special educational needs, such as dyslexia. Additional funding is more usually provided, through statements or otherwise, for less common but often more difficult to manage needs: the 'low incidence–high impact' needs. However, there are still tensions and debates about whether there is sufficient resourcing or efficient and equitable management of SEN provision. Parents too are more often requesting specialist placements through the Special Educational Needs and Disability Tribunal (SENDIST).

The purpose of this book is to support the SENCo, head teachers, governors, staff and parents by outlining the key aspects of whole-school SEN policy development and to provide help in reviewing progress. Each school will need to make its own decisions about the SEN dilemmas and how to resolve them in relation to local priorities and resources. When reviewing the school's SEN and disability policy and practice, it may be useful to begin by reflecting on the changes in perspective about children with disabilities that have been described in this chapter. Some questions to ask might be:

- How have the legacies of the past affected our present concepts of special educational needs and disability?
- How important is the language used to describe pupils' difficulties?
- How has power in decision-making changed over the years in relation to pupils with SEN? Who has the greatest power now?
- How have parent and pupil rights changed?
- What changes have been seen in your own school, over the last ten years, in relation to SEN and disability provision and practice?

CHAPTER 2

Roles and Responsibilities within Whole-school SEN Coordination

This chapter introduces the theme of roles and responsibilities in mainstream schools for pupils with special educational needs. This includes the roles and responsibilities of the governors and head teacher, as well as those of the SENCo. The overall responsibilities lie with the governing body and the head teacher, who carry out the strategic planning for the school's development. All teachers have a responsibility for those pupils in their classes with special educational needs. Parents, pupils and ancillary staff also have their parts to play. The coordination of the day-to-day policy and practice for SEN is the responsibility of the SENCo. It is important to conceptualise all of the above as part of a whole-school approach to SEN coordination.

Effective schools manage special educational needs by being clear about their priorities when allocating roles and responsibilities. Effective school policies also depend on good communication systems between all those holding these responsibilities. The school moves forward in its development by integrating special needs policies into the School Improvement Plan as a whole. Effective schools remain so by being reflective organisations which manage change. This requires a mixture of flexibility and consistency. The challenge of SEN is that of constant change and the necessity to adapt not only to the needs of the pupils but also to new legislation or ways of allocating resources.

The Code of Practice (2001) advises flexibility in the response adopted by schools and early years settings but reminds everyone that they must be able to demonstrate that in the arrangements made for children with SEN, they are fulfilling their statutory duty to have regard to the Code. (See Appendix 2a for Statutory Regulations.)

Whatever arrangements are made in a particular school, statutory duties remain with the governing body. The Code of Practice also uses the term 'responsible person'. This is usually the head teacher, but may be a governor, often the chair, unless the governing body have designated another governor.

Since 1986 the role of governors as responsible authorities in schools has radically changed. Governors have acquired a number of responsibilities in law relating to their role as employers of people with disabilities, as providers of education to their disabled pupils and as providers of a service to other disabled users of the school. Governors must, in law, ensure that children and young people have their learning difficulties and disabilities (LDD) identified and assessed and that appropriate provision is made for them. The day-to-day management of this often falls to the SENCo who needs to ensure good recording systems are in operation. The law also requires governing bodies to publish and report on the success of their SEN policy and practice each year. (See Appendix 2b Governors Responsibilities. Theme continues in Chapter 10.)

School responsibility for disability

Partly as a result of the persistent lobbying of the Disability Rights Commission (DRC), Part 4 of the Disability Discrimination Act (DDA 1995) was further amended, to introduce powerful and practical duties upon schools. All schools, like all other public bodies, now have a general disability equality duty to:

- promote disability equality
- eliminate discrimination against disabled people
- eliminate discrimination and harassment of disabled people
- promote positive attitudes towards disabled people
- encourage participation by disabled people in school and public life
- take steps to meet disabled peoples needs even if this requires more favourable treatment.

Schools have three areas of responsibility:

- as employers
- as providers of education to pupils
- as providers of services to parents/carers and the community.

They have specific duties to review their employment practices and their systems and provision, including admissions, the curriculum, behaviour and discipline policies and all other aspects of school life to ensure that they are not discriminating against people with disabilities and learning difficulties.

The DRC Code of Practice for Schools (2002a; 2002b) gives practical advice on how to avoid discrimination against disabled pupils and prospective pupils. The examples relate to aspects of school education that are covered by Part 4 of the Act, namely admissions, education and associated services and exclusions. This Act and Code apply to all schools in England, Scotland and Wales including independent and publicly funded mainstream nursery, primary and secondary, and special schools.

> The duty on schools to make reasonable adjustments is anticipatory. It is the potential for a substantial disadvantage that should trigger a consideration of what reasonable steps might need to be taken. Schools cannot, in general, wait until a disabled pupil has arrived before making reasonable adjustments. This may be too late and it may not be possible to take reasonable steps before the pupil is placed at a substantial disadvantage.
> (DRC Code of Practice for schools 2002a; 2002b: 6.12)

> The reasonable adjustments duty is owed to disabled children in general, not simply to individual disabled children.
> (DRC Code of Practice for schools 2002a; 2002b: 6.13)

All schools were required, by December 2007, to have drawn up a Disability Equality Scheme (DES) which shows what they have done, and will do, over a three-year period to increase access and involvement and to improve outcomes for disabled people. They must:

- consult disabled staff, pupils, parents and carers (themselves disabled and of disabled pupils) governors and to others in the community;
- actively review their policies and practices and assess the impact of these on people with disabilities and learning difficulties;
- plan improvements;
- publish an action plan;
- review outcomes annually, learning as much from what doesn't work as from what does, and revise the scheme formally after three years.

Excellent advice on implementing the DDA and drawing up a Disability Equality Scheme has been published (DfES 2006b) and at www.drc-gb.org. The schemes will be inspected and monitored for their efficacy.

The implication of this Act and its Code are clear; in future schools must develop policy and practice which will prevent unlawful or discriminatory practice. This is a whole-institution issue and one to which the SENCo can contribute. However, SENCos cannot be held individually responsible for school policy and practice.

The role of the Special Educational Needs Coordinator

The role of the SENCo and the concept of a whole-school policy for special educational needs have been developing over the years since 1983. All maintained schools now accept that they have responsibilities for special needs and that someone has to be named as their SENCo, even though that role may well be doubled and trebled with other roles held by that person. Independent schools are also becoming more aware of these responsibilities and many are appointing SENCos and developing SEN policies. The inclusion agenda is also part of schools' responsibility and some schools prefer to appoint an Inclusion Coordinator (INCO) in recognition of the broader range of pupils such as those with English as an Additional Language (EAL) or possibly disaffected pupils.

It is now recognised by the government that the role of the SENCo has become more challenging, requiring strategic leadership. In Early Years settings, both site and area SENCos are now appointed. The Education and Inspections Act (DfES 2006a) introduced changes to the 1996 Education Act in response to concerns of the Education and Skills Select Committee (July 2006). Governing bodies have a duty to designate a member of staff to coordinate provision for pupils with SEN. It is also stated that the SENCo should be a teacher and should have a seat on the school's Senior Leadership Team (SLT). It is recognised that knowledge, skills and experience will be required. The TDA professional development plan for 2008–11 indicates that in future, newly appointed SENCos will be required to undertake nationally accredited training (www.tda.gov.uk/teachers/continuingprofessionaldevelopment.aspx).

Every Child Matters: Change for Children (DfES 2004a) identifies that pupil performance and well-being go hand-in-hand. Cheminais (2005) says that children and young people cannot learn if they do not feel safe or if health problems create barriers. This means that while tracking pupil progress, by means of achievement targets or tests, it will be equally important to ask pupils and parents about the quality of life in school. The Standards Agenda requires schools to carry out testing, which in turn may lead to stress in some pupils or disaffection in others. Innovative and inclusive practice must therefore balance the push for results, with the total well-being of pupils and staff. SENCos have their part to play, usually focusing on those with identified LDD. SENCos manage a range of personnel and liaise with parents and professionals from outside agencies. SENCos also help their schools become more effective as learning communities. (The theme of SENCo role is continued in Chapters 6, 9 and 10.)

Time as a resource

In primary schools many SENCos are also full-time class teachers or may hold other responsibility posts. In secondary schools the SENCo may head the SEN department or be a subject teacher for part of the time. Of vital importance is communication between all parts of the system. The head teacher should allocate time for liaison and planning between everyone involved, for the SENCo to see parents and to meet other agencies. The policy must make it clear who is responsible for each aspect of the work. The referral and information systems of the school should also be clear to all users, including the parents. (The theme is continued in Chapters 6, 9 and 10.)

The Code of Practice (2001) suggests that the role of the SENCo is at least equivalent to a curriculum coordinator in a Primary school or a head of year, or the head of department in a secondary school. The Code says that: 'Governing bodies and head teachers will need to give careful thought to the SENCos' timetable in the light of the Code and in the context of the resources available to the school' (Code of Practice: 5.10).

The National Union of Teachers SEN survey (2004) asked many questions about SENCo non-contact time. As in previous surveys, the picture is complex, depending on school size and population and other roles the SENCo holds. The amount of time allocated ranged from a full timetable to 2–4 hours a week. The reasons given for insufficient non-contact time were ranked as follows: school priorities lie elsewhere; lack of finance and other commitments (teaching and non-teaching). For this reason the amount that any one SENCo can be expected to achieve will vary from school to school.

Leading, managing and training staff

The Code of Practice (2001) states that the responsibilities of a SENCo will include:

- overseeing the day-to-day operation of the school's SEN policy
- co-coordinating provision for children with special educational needs
- liaising with and advising fellow teachers
- managing learning support assistants
- overseeing the records of all children with special educational needs
- liaising with parents of children with special educational needs
- contributing to the in-service training of staff
- liaising with external agencies including the LEA's support and educational psychology services, health and social services, and voluntary bodies.

One aspect of the SENCo role which has developed and is now fully recognised in the Code of Practice (2001), is that of leading, managing and training of support staff. Since the 1990s there has been a large increase in the number of additional staff working in schools (see Chapter 6). *The National Standards for SENCos* (TTA 1998: 13) stated that SENCos should take an active part in leading and managing staff. Specifically they should:

> Advise, contribute to and, where appropriate, co-ordinate the professional development of staff to increase their effectiveness in responding to pupils with SEN, and provide support and training to trainee and newly qualified teachers in relation to the standards for the award of Qualified Teacher Status, Career Entry Profiles and standards for induction.
>
> (National Standards for Special Educational Needs Co-ordinators, TTA 1998: 13)

The SENCo as an agent for change

The pressure on schools to become more inclusive in meeting the needs of a wider range of pupils; to consider the five principles of ECM and to keep excellent records, could feel overwhelming.

SENCos are asking teachers to change their practice when improving the teaching and learning for pupils with SEN. SENCos in turn are being asked as part of the school team to think strategically in terms of systems, planning and staff development. When SENCos have their place on the SLT and are fully supported by their head teacher it may be possible for them to manage change.

> What seems inescapable is that change will continue to impact on SEN and inclusive practice at a rapid rate in the future. This necessitates that SENCos should feel confident about implementing changes in their own schools.
>
> (Cowne and Robertson 2005: 31)

Layton (2005) reconceptualises the TTA's version of the core purposes of SENCos, in collaboration with the head teacher – 'as to lead staff in creating the conditions that favour the participation and learning of all pupils'. In her article she continues to analyse the leadership aspect of the role, arguing that though personal qualities are essential to effective leadership, the condition in which this occurs must also be part of the picture. It will only be when SENCos are fully supported by their school leaders that they can be effective change managers.

An individual SENCo can only manage so much change. It is therefore essential to judge what can be done at any one time and in each setting. O'Hanlon (1993) comments that special needs work is often carried out in 'occupied territory' and the role requires 'barter, negotiation and compromise'. Organisations vary, but within most there will be in-built resistance to change. This may come from one member of staff or from nearly everyone. The more resistance there is the more carefully and slowly it will be necessary to proceed. Why is change resisted? It may be due to a lack of knowledge or competence which induces feelings of fear of failure. This can be avoided by giving time and opportunities for discussion and support, and building-in time for liaison and planning meetings. (See Critical Incident Analysis Activity 1, which helps focus on emotional issues when managing change.)

Practitioner research as a tool for change

O'Hanlon confirms that qualitative practitioner research provides the foundation for individual and institutional change. She says that

> critical enquiry within the school empowers the teacher researcher, and it allows the special needs teacher to share evidence, discuss issues and engage in reflective decision-making with colleagues.

> (O'Hanlon 1993: 103)

Practitioner research can be one way of starting the change process, giving all those involved an opportunity to innovate change and evaluate and reflect on the results. This is often undertaken as part of a training course. This examination can begin with a review of existing practice or policy within the chosen area. Once the area or problem which needs solving or improving has been chosen, further information is collected. This in turn leads to a choice for an innovation or change.

Developing and maintaining a whole-school approach

Developing these roles and coordinating the whole-school approach will evolve over time. Schools will be at different stages of development in this process, therefore it is important to evaluate what each school has achieved. The next step may be to check staff understanding and knowledge of school SEN policy and evaluate what each believes

(a) *should* be the policy
(b) is *actually* the case at present (see Activity 2 – The Audit).

Policy means intended action. But it is based on a value system which may mean changing the attitudes of some or all staff, and such change takes time. Each year, the policy must be evaluated against the success criteria of the previous year (see Figure 2.1).

Self-evaluation and school improvement

In 2003 Ofsted revised their inspection framework and gave high priority to self-evaluation. They also made evaluation of inclusion a part of the inspection framework.

> The purpose of self-evaluation is to provide a coherent framework located within overall planning systems and well aligned to other principal features of the improvement process.
> (Aspect 2005)

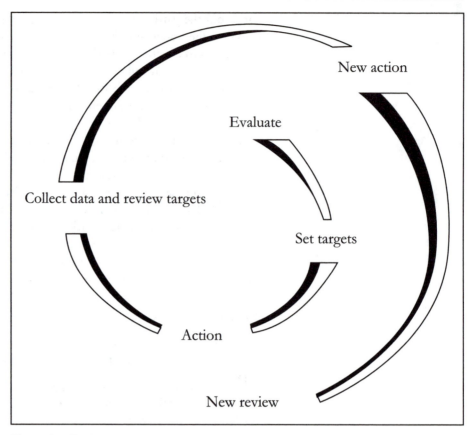

Figure 2.1 Review cycle

SENCos who are members of the SLT should be involved in this process and make sure that SEN is not sidelined. They also may wish to select aspects of provision for improvement as part of the ongoing cycle of evaluation of the SEN policy. The Self Evaluation Form (SEF) gives schools an opportunity to focus on a particular aspect of their work. This could give SENCos an opportunity to include SEN issues and provide information about provision. The process of SEF is vital to help strategic planning and efficient use of resources.

Data analysis

Pupil performance data from subject leaders (in secondary schools) or class teachers in primary schools will help build a picture of individual learning strengths, weaknesses and levels of independence.

> The point of gathering all this information, is to identify clearly the next steps in learning for pupils. School management teams, including SENCos, must together establish:
>
> - What information most helps teachers track children's progress
> - How best to collect and analyse information
> - How to use the analysis to evaluate and adjust the teaching and lesson design to meet individual needs.
>
> (Key Stage 3, National Strategy 2004)

(For further information see www.standards.gov.uk or DfES/0148/2004.)

Monitoring and evaluation

Part of SEN coordination is the monitoring and evaluation on a regular basis of the school's SEN policy and practice. Monitoring may be led by the SENCo or by members of the senior leadership team. If targets in the previous year have been set using success criteria and clear performance indicators then it will be easy to see what has been achieved. It is important, therefore, when choosing targets as part of the School's Improvement Plan (SIP) to:

1. make these small and precise enough to be achieved
2. set criteria or indicators so that success can be recorded or lack of success investigated
3. allocate roles and responsibilities for the implementation of the target
4. set a time-scale on implementation
5. evaluate how successful the school was in reaching this target.

This means that at the end of each year the policy must be evaluated and new targets decided for the following year along with some new success criteria. The review needs to ask:

- Were last year's targets reached?
- Have changes to provision or policy been made?
- Have any roles and responsibilities changed significantly or new people been appointed?
- Has the LA policy changed in any way which will influence school policy? (For example, have SEN funding arrangements changed?)

(See Activity 6 for practice in setting success criteria for a target area of policy.)

Developments and changes in the school's policy and practice must be made known to the governing body by the head teacher or SENCo, and the governors must include this information in their annual report to parents. If the policy is to remain active and dynamic, it must be seen as a process of development. This requires maximum involvement of the head teacher and senior management team, representation from the curriculum and pastoral systems, as well as the coordination of practice by the SENCo. If effective, the whole-school policy is likely to enhance the teaching, learning and well-being of *all* pupils. The SEN policy needs to be seen as part of the School's Improvement Plan (SIP) and to link with other existing policies such as those for equal opportunities or behaviour. There should also be a strong relationship to the assessment policy and to curriculum planning. (See Activity 6.)

> Regulations made under Section 42 of the School Standards and Framework Act 1998 require that the governing body's annual report *must* include information on the implementation of the governing body's policy on pupils with special educational needs and any changes to the policy during the last year.
>
> (Code of Practice, DfES 2001b: 1.28)

The SEN budget

Schools have additional funding allocated from the LA for funding SEN. This may be given in relation to a variety of indicators, of which the most common is the number of pupils who are eligible for free school meals. In some LAs funding for pupils with statements has also been delegated. Schools are accountable for the proper use of all these funds. This means senior management and governors should set an SEN budget and make it known how resources have been allocated 'between and amongst' all those identified as having SEN. It is up to the school to decide how it will apportion all funds except those earmarked for statements.

The National Union of Teachers (NUT) survey (2004) found that schools lacked the necessary expertise in issues related to SEN funding. The survey said that greater clarity was required so that head teachers and SENCos know the exact amount provided and how to use it appropriately. Schools may use money from the general age/pupil weighted unit (APWU) as well as money in the additional needs fund, but SEN must be a clearly identified budget heading.

> The National Standards for SENCos states clearly that 'SENCos identify with the support of the head teacher and governing body, appropriate resources to support the teaching of pupils with SEN and monitor their use in terms of efficiency, effectiveness and safety'.
>
> (National Standards for Special Needs Co-ordinators, TTA 1998 : 14)

Experience shows that many SENCos do not feel empowered to become involved in policy and resourcing issues. They may not have access to information or feel they can ask for it. In these cases, the strategic SEN coordination is in the hands of the head and governors. It will be important for the SENCo to ensure that the head teacher and governing body has up-to-date information about the numbers of pupils at each of the graduated stages of the Code and the provision made to support them. Provision mapping can be an efficient way of demonstrating the range of additional and different types of support given and what it costs. Costing will usually be annual, although termly updates may be necessary when the school population is transient. (See Activity 4.)

Inclusive school systems

Schools can be defined as open systems, which include parents and communities. Some schools can include more of their community within the school than others. This depends on the knowledge, competence and confidence of staff and on effective policies of support and communication. It also depends on the value-system of the governors and senior management team and how these pervade the whole school. It is said that a school that is effective for pupils with SEN is usually effective for all pupils. Such a school will support staff and parents' needs as well as those of the pupils. It will run efficiently and standards and expectations will be high. Such a school is likely to have a more inclusive policy for pupils with problems or differences. (This theme of inclusion continues in Chapter 11.)

CHAPTER 3

Identification, Assessment and Planning for Progress

Identification of those with Special Educational Needs (SEN)

The Education Act (1996) defined children as having special educational needs if they had a learning difficulty significantly greater than the majority of those of the same age. The Code of Practice (DfES 2001b) further clarified this to say that only those children for whom it was necessary to take some additional or different action to enable the pupil to learn more effectively, should be considered to have special educational needs. Two of the main duties of the SENCo, as stated in the Code of Practice (DfES 2001b), are to:

1. oversee the records of all children with SEN
2. coordinate the provision for children with SEN.

Thus the starting point of all work in SEN is the identification of pupils who may have additional or different needs. These pupils' needs will be met through the graduated response as given in the Code of Practice (DfES 2001b). Once a pupil has been identified, information gathering and assessment take place and this contributes to a planned intervention aimed at reducing barriers to learning or access to the curriculum. SENCos have a major role in advising and supporting staff over such planning. Part of this process will be to collect data about an individual child using existing records, including assessments carried out as part of normal school practice.

The Code of Practice (2001) regulations state that the SEN policy must explain the school's identification, assessment, monitoring and review procedures, including the graduated assessment procedures. Those with statements for SEN, for whom the school is responsible, must have annual reviews. To warrant a description of SEN a child will have learning difficulties which cause concern over time, probably to both parents and teachers. Such a child is not responding as expected to the curriculum on offer or cannot cope within the normal classroom environment without additional help. The Code of Practice encourages all class teachers to raise any concerns they may have, usually with the SENCo, who will make the decision about which children have sufficient or appropriate needs to require additional provision. Whilst all children have individual needs, these are not necessarily related to learning difficulties or disabilities as defined by the 1981 or 1996 Acts. There are some children for whom the definition of SEN may not be appropriate.

English as an additional language

Children for whom English is not their first language may still be developing their bilingual ability. At the early stages of this process, access to the curriculum, as delivered, is difficult. These children do not necessarily have learning difficulties;

indeed they may be very efficient learners. If these learners are at the early stages of learning English they should *not* be considered as having SEN. Hall writes:

> Some pupils whose first language is not English will need support to extend their speaking and writing repertoires and to practise new words and phrases in a relevant context. Schools must however ensure that lack of English proficiency is not assumed to indicate SEN or learning difficulties.
>
> (Hall 2001: 78)

The Code of Practice states:

> Lack of competence in English must not be equated with learning difficulties. At the same time, when children who have English as an additional language make slow progress, it should not be assumed that their language status is the only reason; they may have learning difficulties.
>
> (Code of Practice, DfES 2001b: 5.16)

Speaking to the child's parents is advisable in order to understand their perception of the child's progress. It will be important to find out how long the child has been learning English and how the child functions using their home language. It should be possible to arrange assessment in the child's own language through local services. Pupils should be encouraged to use their own language as well as English (see Appendix 3).

Able pupils

Able or gifted pupils need a differentiated curriculum. Their needs should be identified and met by providing opportunities for extension and problem-solving, and a challenging delivery of the curriculum. Schools should have a separate policy for able and gifted pupils, and curriculum planning which takes account of such pupils. They do *not* however have learning difficulties and should *not* be seen as having SEN. However, there may be gifted children who have other problems or disabilities. In these cases there will be other reasons for considering their needs for monitoring and further assessment. This is particularly the case when performance changes and is not what was previously expected. Montgomery reminds us that,

> gifted pupils with special needs exist and are more widely found than perhaps expected . . . the most obvious sign of difficulty is the special need; the other, the giftedness, is regarded as a bonus, but they can cancel each other out.
>
> (Montgomery 2003: 5)

Decision-making and the continuum of need

There is a continuity of need between what is perceived as special or normal. The graduation is such that the cut-off point can appear arbitrary. The decision as to where to draw this line is made by a range of individuals and organisations. All of these have differing perspectives about their priorities, which depend on their knowledge and their value systems. This presents one of the dilemmas of special educational needs. Schools may have different constructs of the term 'special educational needs', which then relate to different priorities about how to use available resources to meet these needs. Schools vary greatly in the proportion of their pupils they consider to have special educational needs. Research has, over the years, shown that approximately 18–20 per cent, or up to one-fifth of a school population are considered as having some SEN. Croll and Moses found in 2000 that teachers considered 1 in 4 pupils to have some level of SEN. If a school identifies a significantly higher proportion, for example 40 per cent, then questions should be asked as to whether it is sensible to conclude that such a large proportion of pupils have significant additional needs? Would it not be better to consider other ways of delivering the curriculum to this population?

Decisions on the following points need writing into the school's policy in the identification section. Who will be involved in early identification?

- *the SENCo*: needs to know the name and basic information to begin record keeping
- *the class/subject teacher*: in order to plan and maintain records
- *the parents*: so their views can be taken into account and their role in helping can be planned
- the pupils: so their views are also recorded and acted upon.

The SENCo is responsible for ensuring that all those with additional or different needs have been identified and that assessment and planning have been carried out and that progress is reviewed and recorded. Consideration should also be given to disability definitions. The SENCo may also be responsible for listing those needs according to the categories given in the Code of Practice (DfES 2001b: 7.52) (see Appendix 1b).

> Since January 2004, we [DfES] have collected information about the numbers of pupils in the country with different types of special educational need (SEN) as part of Pupil Level Annual Schools Census (PLASC). The data is used to help with planning, to study trends and to monitor the outcomes of initiatives and interventions for pupils with different types of SEN.
>
> (www.teachernet.gov.uk/wholeschool/sen)

Assessment

Our present school population is probably the most tested in the world. The government links the assessment process with their agenda of raising standards. However, the direct link between testing and progress is not clear. Testing pupils does not, in itself, raise standards; it is changes in the teaching and learning process that will do this. Most tests are summative in nature – they are useful for administrative purposes: to collect and compare data and result in teachers being kept under continual pressure to produce 'results'. The type of assessment that has proved to make a difference in enhancing performance is formative in nature. Formative assessment gives feedback to the learner and informs the teacher what and how to teach the next step. But as Black and Wiliam argue:

> The political commitment to external testing of teachers and schools in order to promote competition through league tables has a central priority, whilst the commitment to formative assessment is probably a marginal feature.
>
> (Black and Wiliam 1998: 7)

Formative assessment is a continuous process of monitoring each pupil's performance, noting strengths and weaknesses and planning future lessons in the light of them.

> Whilst it [formative assessment] can help all pupils, it gives particularly good results with low achievers where it concentrates on specific problems with their work, and gives them both a clear understanding of what is wrong and achievable targets for putting it right.
>
> (Black and Wiliam 1998:9)

Learning intentions for all lessons need to be as clear as possible. Clarke (2001) states that the clarity of these are essential and must be shared with the pupils. Research has shown that children are more motivated if they know and understand the learning intentions. But as Clarke says, there is a difference between what teachers want children to do and what they want them to learn. Learning intentions also need to be matched to children's abilities.

Personalised learning

The purpose of introducing the concept of personalised learning was to increase pupil participation and motivation, and to raise standards. It is not about individualising learning for each pupil though this may be necessary for certain pupils, some of the time. The five components of personalised learning are:

1. assessment for learning that feeds into lesson planning and teaching strategies
2. a wide range of teaching techniques to promote a broad range of learning strategies
3. curriculum entitlement and choice
4. organisation of school (e.g. workforce remodelling)
5. partnerships beyond the school.

The most relevant theme for this chapter is Assessment for Learning (AfL). This aims at bringing the locus of control nearer the student, which will affect the intrinsic motivation of the pupil and therefore the will to learn. This reaffirms the case for formative assessment techniques by:

- giving feedback (on the learning process)
- involving students in objective setting and purposes
- using assessment outcome to change teaching
- encouraging students to self-assess
- understanding the criteria used to assess.

(Further details can be found at www.standards.dfes.gov.uk/personalisedlearning.)

When schools have good assessment systems for all pupils, those with additional or different needs are more easily identified. However, more detailed assessment may then be necessary to find out what barriers to learning apply and to develop effective strategies to overcome these.

Special needs assessment models

Special needs assessment has traditionally used two models and purposes. These are the medical model and the curriculum model.

The medical model

The medical model uses a diagnostic approach that produces a label for a disability or difficulty. Originally used by the medical profession, specific physical or sensory impairments were identified, using clinical judgements, sometimes backed by tests. The language of the medical model still uses phrases like diagnosis. remediation and treatment. Certain types of diagnostic testing are helpful in analysing difficulties when used by competent professionals. Category labels may also be used to assign pupils to a specific type of special school or provision. For certain physical and sensory disabilities or those with communication and interaction difficulties, this 'medical model' will be of use in helping to decide types of provision, including therapies. However, when defining needs in the other two categories, cognitive and learning needs, and behavioural, emotional and social development needs, the medical model is less appropriate.

The curriculum model

The curriculum model makes fewer assumptions about the difficulty being 'within child' than the medical model. This model recognises that the teaching and learning process is interactive and that teaching strategies and learning styles have an important part to play in overcoming barriers.

Curriculum based assessment 'took off' in the years between the publication of the 1981 Act and that of the Code of Practice (DfE 1994). Educational Psychologists

(EPs) and LEA advisors ran training courses for teachers, particularly those who had become SENCos, based on behaviourist theories of learning. Using task analysis to break down complex activities into easily learnt steps, meant the child was assessed on what he/she could do, at the same time as being helped to achieve target objectives. Praise was given as each small step was achieved, thus building on success.

The task analysis approach became the platform on which the Individual Education Plan (IEP) was developed following the introduction of the 1994 Code of Practice. Teachers were encouraged to assess children on aspects of learning which were causing concern and set targets to be achieved, stating what type of support strategies would be used. Pupil and parent views were also to be recorded. But writing IEPs became unmanageable and too far removed from the teaching process.

The strength of using a curriculum based approach to assessment is, however, important as it tells us what a child can do and this can then be used to plan the next steps in teaching. If this is combined with monitoring the effects of mediated learning, that is, supporting the child so that they can understand how to learn, then we have a dynamic assessment process. One of the best known examples of this type of assessment was Feuerstein *et al.*'s (1980) Learning Potential Assessment Device (LPAD). Feuerstein considered the task of assessment was to explore the potential for being modified by mediated learning, thus in his model, assessment and teaching are intertwined. Recording a full dynamic assessment is, however, labour intensive, so may only be useful on some occasions and with selected children. But to some extent many teachers make use of this model when working intensively with a child, though they may not record it formally.

Assessment techniques related to Code of Practice (COP) categories

Cognition and learning

Cognitive impairment was typically ascertained by the use of IQ tests usually administered by EPs. On the basis of such assessments, placements for specialist provision were often made. These tests give useful data, but are best when used as part of an on-going diagnostic teaching process which also uses observation of the pupil's strategies (see above). Otherwise the use of such tests can produce a deficit model of need. Such static tests typically give information about selective performance taken on a single occasion. They are also not 'culture fair' for pupils whose language or cultural background is different from that used to standardise the tests. Published attainment tests, largely related to literacy, can be useful tools for teachers (see Source List 1). Wherever possible, read the author's guidance notes to select and score appropriately.

The assessment process will also use data from the National Curriculum Standard Assessment Tests (SATs) and the National Literacy and Numeracy attainment tests. Although these tests give teachers data about the performance of their pupils, they are primarily designed to provide comparative rather than individual data. Children whose development is delayed may not make sufficient progress to register on the National Curriculum levels and be given a 'W' to show they are working towards Level One. For such children, performance (P) scales are a valuable way to address smaller steps of progress. Evidence of participation may be collected through annotated photographs as shown in Buck and Davis (2001). From September 2007, the Department for Children, Schools and Families (DCSF) requires teachers to use the P scales to measure attainment for those pupils who are working below National Curriculum Level 1. As part of the statutory duty, these assessments must be reported by schools. (For more information go to www.pscales.qca.org.uk. and see Source list 1b.)

Children with behavioural, emotional and social difficulties

These pupils are usually identified by teachers, parents and professionals by means of observation of behaviour in and out of the classroom. The medical model is usually inappropriate for the assessment of most pupils with behavioural, emotional and social development needs, though it is often used in the labelling of hyperactive pupils, for example those with Attention Deficit Hyperactive Disorder (ADHD). Many pupils' learning difficulties are caused by their emotional state or by their inability to learn appropriate behaviour. Pupils may be continually off-task, sometimes disrupting others, sometimes only themselves. Such pupils often have low self-esteem and poor learning strategies. Observation, time to talk with the child in a relaxed atmosphere, may pave the way to curriculum based assessment. Good record-keeping for pupils with emotional or behavioural difficulties will note:

- information about the pupil's learning style;
- relationships with peers and adults;
- relevant information from parents about the pupil in the home context;
- the pupil's attitudes to learning (can they risk failure?);
- observation about the pupil's strengths which can be used to build better self-esteem;
- how this pupil can be helped to function more effectively within the class.

Communication and interaction

Assessment of these children is likely to include diagnostic tests carried out either by those from the medical or psychological professions or from teachers who have expertise in the particular area. SENCos should become familiar with the local services from which such help in assessment can be obtained (see Chapter 7). Careful observation, discussions with parents and records of previous development will be of great use in such assessments.

Sensory and /or physical including medical conditions

> Sensory impairment ranges from profound deafness or visual impairment through to lower levels of loss which may only be temporary. Physical impairments may arise from physical, neurological and metabolic causes that only require appropriate access to educational facilities. Others may lead to more complex learning difficulties.
>
> (Code of Practice, DfES 2001b: 7.62)

The majority of children in this category are likely to have been diagnosed prior to starting school, sometimes shortly after birth. However, with lower levels of impairment it may only be in the school environment that the disability emerges. Careful observation by teachers is essential in discovering whether there is such lower-level impairment. Where there is a change in behaviour it is wise to check for sensory or physical difficulties, which if missed, may lead to greater problems. The revised Code (2001) states that the assessment process is fourfold, focusing on:

1. the child's learning characteristics
2. the learning environment
3. the task
4. the teaching style, classroom organisation and differentiation.

(Code of Practice, DfES 2001b: 5.6)

This definition uses a version of the curriculum model, in that the context of learning becomes part of the assessment process. The model also allows for dynamic assessment to take place.

General principles relating assessment to planning

Assessment, for those with significant difficulties, must provide enough detail to help plan carefully so that progress can be made. This will mean an understanding of each disability or difficulty, and the barriers to learning that must be overcome. The total learning context for the pupil must be taken into account. This includes noting relationships with parents and teachers and features related to home and school environments. It is very important to include notes of the child's own view of their learning and the problem they think they may have. Questions to ask of assessment are:

- How does this relate to real classroom activities?
- How does this relate to long-term realistic goals?
- Is what is being tested relevant to the learner themselves and will it enhance or damage their self-esteem?
- Can this type of assessment be carried out within the time available and resources of staff?
- Are cross-curricular skills being assessed?
- Can the pupil access the curriculum on offer?

Planning for those with additional needs

Individual educational plans (IEPs) were first described in the 1994 Code of Practice to improve planning for those on the SEN register. The 2001 Code of Practice refined the use of IEPs in an attempt to simplify their format and to limit their use to only those with additional/different needs. However, this still resulted in IEPs being produced for most on School Action and School Action Plus of the graduated response to the Code of Practice. The result of this was twofold. Firstly, the overload of bureaucracy led to stress on SENCos, and, secondly IEPs became less related to the teaching and learning process and were often largely ignored by class and subject teachers. As planning for all pupils improved and in particular the refinement, known as Waves 1, 2 and 3, was introduced by the literacy and numeracy strategies, writing of IEPs for the majority with SEN became unnecessary. However, those with significant additional needs, such as those with statements, are likely to require an IEP to be maintained.

The Individual Education Plan: its purpose and design

When used, the function of the individual education planning is to collect information, set targets, decide upon strategies and resources for their achievement and review these regularly. Thus the IEP document has two key purposes:

- *the first is educational*: the information is used to inform teaching and day-to-day management of needs;
- *the second is accountability*: a summary document can be given to pupils, parents, teachers and other professionals or administrators who are to provide additional resources or support.

Educational purposes of IEPs

The IEP should provide information of a sufficiently detailed nature in order to produce:

- targets which can be decided on and understood by the pupil
- strategies, by which these targets may be achieved, including levels and types of support
- success criteria by which progress may be assessed and recorded.

This means the IEP is a plan of action, with targets which can be understood by the pupil and his/her teachers and parents. It must be accessible to everyone as a working document which will influence classroom practice, although, for those with statements specialist programmes may sometimes be necessary. Basic information from each IEP must be given to all teachers who may teach the pupil on a 'need to know' basis.

The paperwork will include a summary sheet describing the child's strengths and difficulties and strategies that have been successful to date. Using Information Communication Technology (ICT) will reduce the time required to write IEPs as once information is on the school databases it can be transferred where needed. Before an IEP can be written, information will have been collected about concerns and all base-line or Standard Assessments referred to. Information about the pupil's strengths and interests should also be recorded. This is important, because it is through these strengths, that positive progress will be made. Pupils' views must be sought as well as those of parents, and should influence how the IEP is written.

Accountability purposes of IEPs

For those pupils on School Action of the graduated response, plans can be recorded within normal lesson planning or on Group Education Plans (GEPs). Now that record keeping and target setting is part of normal practice for all pupils, it is very likely that some of this additional recording takes place within normal school practice.

The Implementation Review states that:

Schools do not need to write Individual Education Plans for children with SEN where they have a policy of planning, target setting and recording of progress for *all* pupils as part of personalised learning that:

- identifies learning targets for individual pupils with SEN
- plans additional or different provision from the differentiated curriculum offered to all pupils
- reviews provision in the light of individual pupil outcomes.

Advice on planning is given in the material from the Primary and Secondary National Strategies.

(Implementation Review Statement, 2007 January)

Group Education Plans

GEPs are written into class planning in order to meet the needs of pupils who require similar teaching strategies, for example children who have a specific literacy difficulty. The aim of the GEP is to plan for the curricular needs of this group alongside the planning for the other groups in the classroom. Targets for this group become learning intentions against which the teacher comments on pupil progress. These comments are made on the teacher's plans, both to record progress and indicate the next steps to be taken. This process is *formative assessment*. When the SENCo wishes to review the progress of a child with a GEP, the teacher goes through the learning intentions for the topic or for a half term. If these are well formulated, the teacher will be able to see what the pupil has learnt by listing what he knows, understands, can do, or has experienced. Teacher comments are collated to form a very accurate record of the child's progress. This is a far more accurate description of progress, as it records the learning as it takes place, rather than trying to recall what a pupil has achieved after a period of time, as was the case with IEP reviews. If more formal documentation is required for an annual review, then a top sheet can be added with biographical details of child and previous achievements. When this system is used alongside a provision map, which details the support and interventions a child is receiving, this is very powerful evidence of children's learning.

Provision mapping

Provision management is an 'at a glance' way of showing all the provision a school makes, as well as identifying needs and staff skills required. Costs can be calculated which enable schools to track their SEN spending. This complete picture allows schools to see the impact of their interventions, identify gaps in provision and when linked with assessment, can show the progress pupils make. Interventions will be those that are *additional to* and *different from* the schools' differentiated curriculum. The process of provision mapping is the responsibility of the whole school, not just the SENCo!

Provision mapping is a powerful strategic tool to help schools monitor how inclusive their provision is, the progress pupils are making and the effectiveness of interventions. As part of the government's agenda to promote inclusion, Ofsted (2005) focuses on self-evaluation, and provision mapping enables schools to gather evidence of how well they are doing. Hrekow (2006) identifies seven steps to drawing up a provision map. These are:

1. Audit projected need.
2. Compare projected need with current pattern of provision, identify changes and plan training.
3. Identify available funding.
4. Consider the evidence of what works.
5. Plan the provision for the next year.
6. Track children's progress and monitor impact.
7. Evaluate the effectiveness of your provision.

(See Activity 4.)

The SENCo's role in decision-making

The number of pupils needing *School Action Plus* is often limited by the availability of local resources, which varies considerably across the country. After a period of assessment or support at *School Action Plus* the pupil may well return to *School Action*. Support services, specifically educational psychologists and learning support teachers, can give advice in an informal way or through in-service training. Parents must also be involved at this decision-point in the process.

SENCos are therefore involved in three stages of the graduated response required by the Code of Practice:

- identification of need using normal school procedures – this will be recorded on a SEN Register or similar document
- organising further assessment where necessary
- planning suitable support provision and mapping, and monitoring this
- changing the child's status in the graduated response for SA to SA+ or a statement. If the existing teaching and strategies result in reasonable progress in line with expectations on SA or SA+. If not, further assessment may be required to advise on additional or different strategies for support.

Referral for a statutory assessment

Very few pupils (1 to 2 per cent of the population) will have such severe and persistent difficulties that they cannot cope within mainstream education without significant additional or alternative provision. If the school has carried out all the work at school-based stages and after consultation with the support services and the parents, they all agree to do so, a request is made by the head teacher to the LA for a multi-disciplinary assessment. While this assessment is taking place the pupil will continue to have an IEP, or similar records, in place, which are carefully monitored. Parents may also request an assessment for a statement of need.

The SENCo will then be asked to collect and collate all documentation, IEPs (if used) or alternative evidence. Then, either they or the head will write to the LA making a formal request for a statutory assessment. Most LAs have proformas for such requests. If the LA agrees to the assessment, they have a duty under the Code to carry this out within six months. This may or may not result in a decision by the LA to give a statement, which might result in placement at a special school. If the LA wishes, they can write a 'note in lieu' of a statement, which means the pupil's needs are discussed, but will be met at *School Action Plus*. The draft statement is sent to the parents who can ask for certain changes to be made (for details see Chapter 8 of the Code of Practice, DfES 2001b). If the LA and the parents cannot agree to these changes or there is a dispute over placement decisions, the parent may take the matter to the SENDIST. But often, LAs will attempt to mediate a mutually satisfactory solution to the parents' request.

This chapter has been concerned with the majority of pupils who remain the responsibility of the school and whose needs are met through careful identification, assessment and planning, then by reviewing progress. This assessment and recording process is *every* teacher's responsibility but the SENCo must keep comprehensive records and ensure the review process is carried out thoroughly. In order for this to be possible, the overall planning of time for reviews, the organisation of paperwork, and clear definition of roles and responsibilities needs to be part of the whole-school policy for SEN and to link to the school's assessment policy. The themes of this chapter are continued in Chapter 9.

CHAPTER 4

The Curriculum
Planning for an Inclusive Curriculum

The previous chapter concentrated on identifying, assessing and planning for those with additional/different needs. The Code of Practice suggested an individual approach by its demands for detailed assessment and planning, but this had the effect of adding to the administrative and bureaucratic load on SENCos. The problem for class and subject teachers is that children are not taught as individuals for much of their day, but in social groupings of up to 30 or more. The teaching and learning process is therefore, interactive. Within-child features play their part, but so do classroom organisation and resourcing, modes of curriculum delivery and teacher management style. Some educators, such as Bruner and Vygotsky, think that learning is best conceptualised as a social process, rather than an individual one. Gipps explains that,

> The social constructivist model of learning assumes that knowledge is built up by the child in the form of connected schemata; the child is seen as an agent of his or her own learning activity constructing knowledge.
>
> (Gipps 1992: 3)

One of Vygotsky's key concepts was that of the 'zone of proximal development' (Vygotsky 1978). This describes the gap between what the child can do alone and what they can do with someone who has more knowledge or skill. Gipps further explains that,

> Vygotsky's model suggests that not all tasks should be perfectly matched to the child's current level of development, indeed some tasks should require a shift to the next 'zone of development'. But what is crucial to this idea, is that interaction with another person is essential, whether this person is a teacher or peer, to help move this moving-on process.
>
> (Gipps 1992: 4)

This suggests a key role for the teacher is to build a rich learning community in the classroom. The classroom is also part of the wider community of the school and the district. It must, however, be remembered that influences beyond the school, both locally and nationally, affect the focus of curriculum delivery and its assessment.

The National Curriculum and differentiation

The Code of Practice (DfES 2001b) describes the National Curriculum as a statutory requirement for all maintained schools that sets out the areas and content of learning in each Key Stage. It continues by reminding teachers that differentiation of learning activities within the curriculum framework will help schools to meet the learning needs of all children, and that schools should not assume that children's learning difficulties always result solely or even mainly, from problems within the child. 'A schools own practice make a difference – for good or ill' (Code of Practice,

DfES 2001b: 5.18). Government circulars and documents continually remind teachers that a flexible approach to differentiation is essential to cover the wide range of ability and experience and to take account of personalised learning.

Wragg had a useful way of conceptualising the curriculum. He started with three propositions, which are: that education must incorporate a vision of the future; that there are escalating demands on citizens and that children's learning must be inspired by several influences. This takes him to his final proposition that 'it is essential to see the curriculum as much more than a collection of subjects and syllabuses' (Wragg 1997: 2). This leads him to propose a curriculum with different dimensions, of which the subject dimension is the first, cross-curricular issues the second, and teaching and learning styles the third. This model has much to offer as a way of including developmental and whole-child aspects so necessary for special needs work. Wragg reminded his readers that pupils are partners in the process of change and improvement, as they need to know about how to think and learn so they can become autonomous learners with the ability to work and live in harmonious groups.

Therefore, it must be remembered that the curriculum covers all aspects of learning carried out in school, and is not just the National Curriculum. A broad view of education would be that it is about learning how to learn and to adapt to changing circumstances. This means that SENCos should aim at helping staff make lessons more inclusive, by changing teaching styles to increase pupil participation in the process of learning.

Work is currently being carried out by Qualifications and Curriculum Authority (QCA) to develop a new curriculum framework which will incorporate the five aims of ECM and broaden the view of the curriculum as the entire learning experience. The statutory expectations remain, but the aim of assessment will be shifted towards making teaching and learning more effective, so learners can understand quality and be shown how to improve.

Personalised learning

In Chapter 3, the initiative for personalised learning was introduced, focusing on Assessment for Learning (AfL). Here it is appropriate to extend the discussion to take in the next two components: effective teaching and learning and curriculum entitlement and choice.

According to the DfES Standards website (www.standards.dfes.gov.uk/personalisedlearning.co.uk), the personalised learning agenda is about 'giving every child a chance to be the best they can'. The DfES suggest that this can be done using a variety of approaches such as giving extra support in groups using peer mentoring and other structured groupings. The initiative has been researched by Sebba *et al.* (2007) who found that schools saw learning approaches as endorsing current activities or providing a means to further develop existing ones. An example of this was the reorganisation of TAs and learning mentors to provide more flexible support. Best practice features included pupils taking more responsibility for their learning and pupil 'voice' being embedded across all five components. Personalised learning does not equate with individualised learning but the research identifies this as an issue for further clarification.

Other commentaries on the initiative focus on the need to see it as about motivation and the need to respond to differences in learning styles and pace. It is also about pupil autonomy, over both what they learn, and how it is learned. The aim is to move the locus of control nearer the student and to keep an open dialogue with the learner.

There can be a conflict between the two government agendas of standards and that of personalised learning. Wedell (2005) discusses the necessity of schools achieving flexibility as recognition of pupil diversity. This means overcoming the rigidity of systems arising from the government's Standards Agenda, and in particular the overemphasis on testing.

Learning styles

A learning style is a method particular to an individual that is presumed to be of most benefit to them. It is therefore suggested that teachers access learning styles of their students and adapt teaching to give opportunities for each to have some choice in how they learn. One model emphasises the sensory modalities of incoming stimuli – visual, auditory, kinaesthetic – often known as VAK. If material is presented in a mixed modality, the learner can then choose their favourite route. Too rigid a labelling of students' styles should, however be avoided as, although it is assumed learners have a preferential style, most people use a mixed modality. The theory of learning styles is controversial, for example, Claxton (2005) questions its uncritical use by the DfES in the personal learning agenda.

The DEMOS Paper has relevance to the debate about raising standards and personalised learning. This report asks questions about how teachers can develop student's capacity to learn and whether particular methods work. 'Learning to learn is not a single entity or skill, but a family of learning practices that change ones capacity to learn' (Hargreaves *et al.* 2005: 7). Most involve the use of 'metacognition' which is the capacity to monitor, evaluate, control and change how one thinks and learns. 'Most of what teachers do in helping students to learn consists of strengthening their metacognitive capacity' (Hargreaves *et al.* 2005: 8). There are many different schemes for determining learning styles. The DEMOS Paper asks for a more critical approach to adopting 'packages' of material for which research evidence of validity and reliability is highly variable.

Some alternative ways of thinking about pedagogy

The second half of this chapter looks at ways of conceptualising pupils' learning within a differentiated curriculum. Approaches are discussed which may help focus on learning styles or experiences, rather than attainment levels, within a set content-based curriculum. The approaches discussed cover three ways of thinking about learning: (1) behavioural, (2) cognitive, in particular thinking skills programmes, and (3) affective, considering the emotional needs of the learner.

The influence of behavioural science on SEN Curriculum and pedagogy

Since the 1980s, special needs curriculum planning and pedagogy have been strongly influenced by behavioural theories. Based largely on applied behavioural analysis these are a development of Skinner's operant conditioning theory of learning. Skinner (1974) believed that by manipulating the environment, you could change an organism's behaviour. First you began by deciding on the goal to be reached and then you shaped the behaviour by a system of reinforcement of successive approximations towards that goal. The reinforcement was food (in work with pigeons or rats) but could be praise when working with people! Skinner argued strongly that his 'science of behaviour' could include a world view of how the environment influenced man's behaviour and indeed his culture.

During the 1980s, educational psychologists in particular, promoted an applied behavioural approach to the analysis of learning difficulties and their remediation. As Norwich suggests, this may have been due to a growing dissatisfaction and lack of confidence in the validity of psychometric testing and its relationship to intervention. He further explains that,

> A behaviourist approach discounts what is not directly observable. What the child can do now is what is assessed. It also is concerned with intended outcomes of the learner rather than what the teacher intends to do or present to the learner.
>
> (Norwich 1990a: 90)

Sometimes called precision teaching, this approach had been successful in special schools for those with learning difficulties. Teachers were trained to write precise small step behavioural targets, set success criteria and state under what conditions the learning would take place (i.e. with how much support). This approach, when well executed, *did* break down barriers to learning for some children, who gained both mastery of certain aspects of the curriculum, and confidence which helped change attitudes to other aspects of learning. However, one of the problems with this method was that it was very labour intensive, requiring individual or very small group teaching and preparation. Another problem was that not all types of learning lend themselves to such a prescriptive, teacher-led approach, which also takes little account of individual learning styles or preferences.

The point here is that the outcomes are chosen and predetermined by the teacher and the child 'shaped' towards these outcomes by the process of rewarding successive steps. This is the task analysis approach to teaching that has become firmly embedded in SEN teaching and is visible in the IEP approach of the Code of Practice.

Wedell (1980) encouraged teachers to negotiate with the learner about objectives and to observe the pupils' preferred learning styles. The fear of a mechanistic and technical approach to education remains. So how can the experience of using the behavioural approach continue to be useful to those planning the differentiated curriculum for SEN?

- *Objectives thinking* has led to a clearer conceptualisation of individual priorities and clearer definition of needs.
- *Baseline assessment* has been a useful starting point on which to build specific programmes to overcome barriers to learning.
- *Goal and target-setting*, if carried out in partnership with the pupil and teacher, can increase self-worth and the child's responsibility for monitoring achievement. Evidence can be collected through observation to prove achievement.
- *Planning small steps* to achieve success has proved worthwhile with the developmentally young or where the task is skills based.
- *Individual priorities and goals* can feed forward to inform both curriculum planning and differentiation and help teachers think about appropriate strategies to help pupils meet their targets.

This behavioural model of learning has strongly influenced the way teachers have planned target-setting for those with SEN and now, all pupils. One shortcoming is that, by concentrating only on what can be observed, little account is taken of inner processes of thinking and feeling. Not only does this feel sterile, it discounts huge areas of human activity and culture. The behavioural model also is very 'teacher led', giving only limited autonomy to the pupil. There is therefore an argument for considering alternative approaches to teaching and learning; for example, a model which enhances the cognitive thinking process, through planned teacher mediation.

Cognitive development and thinking skills programmes

Piaget's theories of cognitive development state that a child goes through stages: first, concrete operational, and then, in adolescence, formal operational thinking (Inhelder and Piaget 1958). The debate about Piaget's stages and ages lies outside the scope of the present discussion. Suffice to say that Piaget and others who extended ideas on cognitive development (Bruner 1968; Donaldson 1978) had significant effects on the pedagogy of the primary 'process' curriculum. However, it is the move into formal operational thinking which is most important in secondary education and which may cause problems for those with learning difficulties.

Cognitive interventions based on formal operational thinking

Formal operational thinking emerges during the secondary school years. It is mediated through environmental and social interaction, but is not tied to any particular subject area. The most significant attempt to intervene and change the learning potential of young people of this age group was that of Reuven Feuerstein in the 1950s. Building on a mixture of psychometrics and theories of Piaget and

Vygotsky, Feuerstein evolved a solution to the sociological problem of the new immigrants arriving in Israel. These young people were not able to take places in the traditional education system and were initially labelled as backward.

Feuerstein, a clinical psychologist, challenged both the traditional trust in IQ tests and the view that intelligence was a once and for all endowment. Feuerstein *et al.* (1980) said that the thinking skills we need in order to learn effectively, and are normally absorbed by children as they develop in their family and culture can, if absent, be instrumentally remedied. Feuerstein developed a theory of mediated learning experiences and a programme of structured exercises known as Instrumental Enrichment (IE). Based on an analysis of the cognitive functions required by learners, the IE course consists of 13 instruments, containing between one and two dozen activities and intended to be taught at a frequency of five hours a week, for at least two years. Feuerstein wished this to be free of all traditional school subject matter (Feuerstein *et al.* 1980; and see Appendix 4 for further information).

His work opened up a whole new field of cognitive education which spread beyond Israel to the USA, Canada, South America, Russia and some countries in Europe. In the early 1980s, officers from several LEAs in England visited the United States and on return agreed to train teachers and set up IE projects. Their work was evaluated by a Schools Council publication (Weller and Craft 1983). One project published the materials known as Somerset Thinking Skills (Blagg *et al.* 1988). These materials help pupils to synthesise information, analyse data, and appreciate their own strategies of thinking.

In England, cognitive intervention programmes could not remain free of subject content. Possibly this was due to pressure of time; certainly once the National Curriculum began. Those who developed programmes may also have felt that these would have more validity to teachers, pupils and the public if the results could be measured in improvements in increased attainments in subject assessments. The best researched and most successful was CASE (Cognitive Acceleration through Science), a project led by Shayer and colleagues between 1984 and 1987.

> CASE materials were designed to address individually the schemata of formal operations and incorporate the principles ... into a set of activities whose content was overtly scientific.
>
> (Adey and Shayer 1994)

This project had measurable success which lasted over time, the effects of which could be seen two years later in GCSE results. In their evaluation of their project the authors emphasise the need for this type of intervention to have 'duration and density' if it is to be effective. By duration they mean that it should take place over at least a two-year period. They further comment that it is not packaged materials and activities which give a new method its power, however useful, as a framework. It depends on thorough staff development, which includes knowledge of the theory of the method, demonstration of skills, followed by practice, feedback and coaching on classroom presentation. Only then will mediated learning take place which really raises standards. However, as Norwich says,

> The point is not to advocate Instrumental Enrichment as such, but to illustrate the point that cross-curricula skills may need additional emphasis for some children with SEN.
>
> (Norwich 1990b: 25)

Multiple Intelligences

Gardner (1983) laid out a theory of multiple intelligences critiquing IQ tests which he felt did not capture the full range of human intelligences. Gardner proposes several dimensions of intelligence – Visual, Spacial, Musical, Verbal, Logical/Mathematical, Interpersonal, Intra-personal, Kinaesthetic and Naturalist.

The Multiple Intelligences (MI) theories influenced educational applications, some of which Gardner himself did not intend. The DEMOS Paper (Hargreaves *et al.* 2005) warns that educational developments of such theories should be tested and findings fed back into theory development. Again, what is being recommended is that teachers are cautious and critical of over-simplified applications of such theories. However, MI has proved popular and has helped teachers become more aware of individual differences in learning. This is particularly important for children with additional needs or disabilities.

Lessons to be learnt from cognitive interventions

What then are the lessons that can be learnt from cognitive interventions and cognitive analysis of pedagogy? The answers may be that:

- Underachievement may be due to a lack of suitable strategies for thinking.
- Pupils *can* be taught thinking skills if the *how* of learning is addressed as well as the *what*.
- Thinking skills can be taught through curriculum subjects, where the use of analogy can help concept development.
- When pupils are taught thinking processes, they gain control of their own learning and this increases motivation and self-esteem.

To do all of the above, teachers will need to learn how to:

- Identify the stage of cognitive development reached by a pupil or group.
- Analyse faulty processes of thinking at the input, elaboration and output phases of lessons and understand the component parts of these processes (see Appendix 4).
- Examine the demand of the curriculum content and materials on offer and adapt these to individual needs.
- Mediate learning through group discussions and by direct teaching of strategies to improve thinking processes.
- Teach pupils to reflect on and vocalise their own thinking processes.
- Use accelerated learning modalities

Affective perspectives

Emotional states are an important part of the curriculum for many reasons. Wragg argues that emotional development could be considered as a subject on the curriculum or a cross-curricular issue, and that it certainly is something that pupils and teachers must understand. 'In positive form, emotions offer a stimulation and enhancement to pupils' learning, in negative form they can be a killer of it' (Wragg 1997: 81).

It is important to recognise that many aspects of the curriculum can feed children's emotional growth. Children need help to explore their own feelings and those of others. One way to keep this on the agenda is by becoming more aware of those aspects of the curriculum which help the understanding of the emotions of others, explore the nature of relationships and make sense of how other people overcome obstacles. Opportunities can be given to explore affective responses to particular themes. 'A climate of warmth and support in which self confidence and self esteem can grow and in which pupils feel valued and able to risk making mistakes as they learn without fear of failure' (National Curriculum Council: NCC 1989).

The world of story, poetry, dance and drama, art and music have a therapeutic role to play, as well as being part of the cultural entitlement for all pupils. Sometimes artistic subjects are seen as having lower prestige than subjects which represent instrumental spheres of knowledge, like science, but it is important that areas of understanding which have a personal characteristic are valued to the same degree. It is often through the creative activities that pupils, who were otherwise unremarkable, begin to shine and achieve. Once this happens, the growth in self-confidence can be harnessed for their less favourite subjects. The other virtue of creative subjects or teaching methods is that they allow open-ended outcomes which are not predetermined and pupils' individual achievements can be accepted. Differentiation by outcome is the norm. These aspects of the curriculum can feed the child, enrich language and ideas, and encourage creative and problem-solving responses. They come nearer to the early years experiences of play, especially when taught by enthusiastic teachers.

Hanko (1995) argues that the curriculum can help pupils to understand the human condition and the part emotions play in people's lives. She comments that teachers do not always realise the full potential of the opportunities the curriculum offers to explore feelings and help pupils build their self-worth. She suggests this may in part be because 'teachers have been side-tracked into mistaking surface behaviour management as a sufficient response to behaviour problems'. She adds that, 'accounts of experiences of concern to pupils can be introduced and through discussion children can speak of their own experiences but also explore in general terms what is reflected in the literature provided. Through use of consultancy groups teachers can find ways of linking personal experience to curriculum content' (Hanko 1995: 76). (See Chapter 6.)

O'Brien and Guiney (2001) assert that pupils usually have a range of self-esteems and that an understanding of this complexity will be necessary to teachers in management of emotional differentiation. These authors write about 'self-esteems' to make the concept less negative and more holistic. Learners often have different self-esteems in relation to different activities. For example, a pupil may have low self-esteem in relation to literacy, but high in a sporting activity. This view of self-esteems recognises that individuals will also vary over time, as well as in different contexts. The authors suggest a mapping technique may prove useful to develop emotional differentiation.

Hanko (2003) discusses ways that teachers can be supported in developing a nurturing environment, one which helps children understand their feelings as they relate to others. Approaches such as Circle Time (Mosely 1993) and Circles of Friends (Newton and Wilson 1999), are useful techniques. But most of all, teachers themselves need support in building confidence to act on competence they already have.

All of the above takes place within the social context of the classroom. Managing this environment so that it produces a positive influence on pupils' thinking, feeling and learning is *the* key skill of the teachers. The environment must be flexible enough to foster learning and support autonomy and structured enough to give security to pupils and to set boundaries. Effective classrooms set within effective schools will support all pupils, but especially those with SEN. Fundamental to all of this is a whole-school culture and ethos which values individuals and allows everyone, teachers and pupils alike, to contribute to the learning process. It must be recognised that emotional and social factors affect all learning, and connections between feelings, reasoning and learning should be developed as a whole-school policy.

The SENCo's role in developing an inclusive curriculum

Increasing participation

Cowne (2003) argues that the challenge to teachers is to increase participation in learning for all pupils. This will require knowledge and understanding of each pupil's existing skills such as being able to listen, follow instructions, problem-solve and understand concepts. When young children enter the school system they are usually eager to learn. However, they may experience a sense of failure or frustration if they can't do a task or don't understand exactly what is required, or because they are not given enough time and no longer feel in control of their learning. Fear of failure can 'creep in' and a continued sense of failure then leads to a reduction in motivation, resulting in either passive learners or those who choose to 'act up' as a diversion for learning. It is important to check that lack of motivation does not arise from unrecognised disabilities or unmet needs. There may be reasons that are triggered by emotional insecurity or differences in home/school cultures. Perceptions from a variety of sources, including those of the child, their family, and other professionals, are needed to build up a picture of the learning situation for this individual. Increasing participation is also about having a positive learning environment with choice available to pupils in terms of tasks, resources, approaches and pace. It is also necessary to recognise what participation can encompass for some pupils. Perhaps an individual cannot fully complete all tasks but may be able to show enjoyment of the experiences of the classroom.

Developing positive learning environments

For any curriculum to be delivered effectively, a positive learning environment is essential. This in turn requires pupils to fit in with normal classroom routines and rules and to respect the rights of others. Certain pupils with learning or behavioural, emotional or social difficulties present a challenge to teachers. It is outside the scope of this section to explore class management in depth. The important point to remember is that curriculum aims include the promotion of spiritual, moral and cultural development of all children. It follows that helping children learn how to work in a harmonious way, so that everyone is respected and valued, is part of the entitlement curriculum.

Develop a learning institution which is responsive to feedback

This means making full use of records and assessment information, to plan schemes of work and lessons. In many cases this will require detailed knowledge of individual pupils and their progress, which may come best from learning support staff and their observations, and from listening to pupil views (see continuation in Chapter 10). At a strategic level this requires liaison time to be built into the timetable so that effective planning can take place concerning delivery of the curriculum. The DRC Code (2002a) makes it clear that schools have a duty to ensure equality of access to the curriculum; as this is a right of all pupils. For the SENCo to be effective in educational, rather than administrative terms, is therefore a challenge. But it could be argued that it is only when those with detailed knowledge of individual differences and learning styles meet with those who plan and deliver lessons, that changes to teaching and learning will occur.

Involve the parents and pupils in the curricular planning process

Parents are very aware that schools should remember individual needs when planning curriculum delivery. Parents of pupils with complex needs often have different priorities for their child. These concern personal, social and life skills. Parents can also problem-solve and have particular roles to play as they see their child from a different perspective than that of the teachers. Parents can remind teachers to think in a cross-curricular way so that the child is not totally overwhelmed or confused by different approaches to topics. Schools now must consider how they are planning to include an important element of Every Child Matters (ECM) – being healthy. The curriculum and its delivery may produce stress for some pupils which could be unhealthy. For example, too much, or unsuitable homework may cause pupils and parents to spend too long on this task. Some pupils react adversely to change and need preparation which parents can provide if they are involved early enough. Parents know, for example, how long ordinary tasks like eating and dressing can take for some children with complex disabilities. All of these types of information can be used when planning for individuals, but may have more general implications for school policies (see Wedell 2006).

Develop a team approach to curricular planning

Support is often the method of differentiation most often chosen for special educational needs work. Support can be conceptualised as support for the pupil, but also as curriculum support with the class teacher. Best practice is when support personnel and teachers work as a team. The team can be extended to include visiting specialists, such as peripatetic teachers and therapists for those with more complex needs. The role of this team is to be as creative as possible in integrating the special requirements of the individual into normal class delivery of the curriculum. Other pupils often enjoy doing activities or games which may originally have been designed for an individual with special needs. The learning community of the classroom will support a wealth of diversity itself, if flexibly managed and democratically controlled. When pupils have joint purposes with teachers they can carry forward individuals whose needs may be quite great and who on their own would struggle to make any progress.

Review resources regularly

Some pupils will have additional resources to help them access the curriculum. Some of these are technical in nature. Equipment must be kept in good condition, with spare parts and switches available. Pupils may need training to use this equipment efficiently, for example, keyboard skills may need to be taught by a suitable instructor. Staff will need training to use aids or to develop ICT activities.

Concluding thoughts

The above sections have been included to give food for thought when planning intervention programmes or thinking of different ways of delivering the curriculum to motivate learning. Clearly, most curriculum planning and development of pedagogy and resources are issues for whole-school development. SENCos can use their particular skills and knowledge, their depth and breadth of understanding of curriculum issues to:

- Draw attention to pupils' individual differences and abilities, including their *strengths*, which build on the pupil's *strengths* and *real-world experiences*. Have high expectations for those with additional needs.
- Remind colleagues that, for many pupils, the role of the teacher is to mediate learning so that the pupil makes connections between their previous experience and the new material.
- Remind teachers that they should remain in charge of the curriculum delivery for those with additional needs and not leave this task to be carried out by TAs on their own.
- Help the school to work pro-actively to meet the needs of pupils by being a *change agent* for curriculum planning.

The next chapter gives some further practical guidance about the SENCo's role in relation to differentiating each of the Key Stages of the National Curriculum.

CHAPTER 5

The Curriculum
Key Issues for Key Stages

This chapter looks at some of the characteristic features of the curriculum within each phase of education. Suggestions are made about the SENCo's role in helping colleagues plan and deliver a differentiated 'Programme of Study' facilitating inclusive education for all pupils, including those with SEN.

Early years (0–5 years)

The main characteristic of the early years curriculum is that it is firmly based on the knowledge of children's development. Play is given a prominent place, but play which is structured to encourage intellectual, social, aesthetic and physical development. The environment of the nursery should be stimulating – encouraging exploration, questioning, experimentation and problem-solving. The adults, set up and mediate the learning experiences of the child, often by engaging in conversation which promotes the child's use of language. Stories and rhymes extend the child's repertoire of language experience into the world of symbolic representation.

Because meeting the individual differences in development is part of an early years practitioner's skills, almost every child with SEN should easily be included. When joining the reception class, children should have a wide vocabulary, be keen to learn and take on the challenge of beginning reading and number work. Research by Tizard and Hughes (1984) shows that early experiences at home and nursery affect the skills children have on entering school. Impoverished experience predisposes children to have more difficulties with school subjects.

There are two main groups of SEN typically found in nursery and reception classes. The first group includes children whose needs were identified pre-school, by parents and health professionals. They may have physical or sensory impairment or be significantly delayed in all round development. Many of this group will have programmes already devised by a range of professionals.

The second group are those whose needs emerge during the early years of schooling. Typical of this group are children with speech and language difficulties, or those whose social skills are poorly developed and who find conforming to group situations very difficult. For behaviour problems, support from educational psychologists may be appropriate. Speech and language therapists are in short supply and usually see children outside school at clinics, although collaborative schemes are being developed in some areas.

The Code of Practice (DfES 2001b) offers advice on Early Years settings in Chapter 4. The Early Years Development and Childcare Partnerships (EYDCP) bring together a diverse range of early years provision which becomes eligible for government funding. All of these settings are required to have regard to the Code of Practice (DfES 2001b) and the DRC Code of Practice (2002a; 2002b). From

September 2008, there will be a statutory framework for the Early Years Foundation Stage (0–5), which sets standards for learning, development and care for children from birth to five. This will apply to all schools and Early Years Ofsted registered settings. The aim of the framework is to help achieve the EMC outcomes by:

- setting standards for learning, development and care for all children from birth to five
- provide equality of opportunity
- create partnership between parents and professionals
- improve quality and consistency across settings
- lay foundations for future learning.

The learning and development requirements are similar to the earlier foundation guidance from the QCA (2000), which provides advice on six areas of learning:

1. personal, social and emotional development
2. communication, language and literacy
3. mathematical development
4. knowledge and understanding of the world
5. physical development
6. creative development.

At the end of the Early Years Foundation Stage, practitioners are required to compile an EYPS profile for each child using observation and assessment in all six areas of learning and development.

> Children with SEN may be working before the level of these assessment goals and require an alternative approach to assessment. In this case providers may use the assessment systems of their LA or others according to the needs of the children.
>
> (DCSF Statutory Guidance 2007b: 2.23–17)

It must be remembered that the style of learning at this age should take into account the needs of the developing child. Development may be slower in some areas. This does not in itself constitute a special educational need.

The role of the early years SENCos

- Working with parents to establish firm partnerships as early as possible, ensuring liaison between parents and a variety of agencies whom offer advice and devise specialist programmes.
- Advising and supporting early years practitioners. This includes the early identification for pupils whose needs emerge in these years.
- Ensuring that appropriate recording of progress and on-going assessment takes place.
- Training TAs and others who work with teachers to support children with SEN.

Key Stage 1: years 5–7

Much of what is true of early years education continues to be true for Key Stage 1. There is the added pressure to meet the demands of the National Curriculum, in particular of teaching literacy and numeracy. A priority will be identifying literacy difficulties early and building in extra support through use of peer and parent partnership programmes.

A broad balanced curriculum

Children continue to need stimulating, enriching experiences that challenge them to ask questions, explore and think. Concepts are developed through structured play, drama, creative activities, as well as through exposure to stories and poetry. It will be important to find which areas of the curriculum enhance the pupil's self-esteem and give opportunities to show their strengths. Classroom organisation, effective use of groups and any adult help available are the keys to meeting individual and special needs in this age group.

For all pupils it is important to remember the link between learning and emotional needs. Friendships are very important to pupils at this age. Personal and social education has a critical part to play in helping children become aware of others' perspectives. A popular development is the use of 'circle time', which aims to help children develop self-esteem, social skills, and the ability to see others' perspectives.

Key issues for SENCos and class teachers

- Ensure detailed recording of literacy and numeracy progress, noting children's preferred strategies.
- Try to prevent children developing feelings of failure when tackling tasks which they find difficult.
- Remember that children need language enrichment; opportunities to talk or listen to stories and share books with an adult in small groups.
- Provide sufficient and varied resources to meet individual needs: a range of suitable books, tapes, computer software, and interactive whiteboards.
- Address classroom management issues and the structure of curriculum delivery to maximise teacher and adult interaction with pupils and to encourage pupil independence.
- Support positive relationships, which enhance self-esteem of pupils by giving value to individual achievement, and encouraging listening activities like 'circle time'.
- Remind teachers that children develop at different rates. Also remember that summer-born children are often at an earlier stage of development and will continue to need the activities of the early years stage to be available. They may have developmental, not special, needs.
- Work closely with parents to keep them informed but also to involve them as much as possible.

(For further information about resources and for further reading that relates to the above, see Source Lists.)

Key Stage 2: junior years 7–11

The demands of the curriculum increase during these years, which may make a child-centred approach more difficult. The characteristics of these junior years is that pupils with moderate or specific learning difficulties and those on the Autistic Spectrum Disorder (ASD) spectrum become more visible, along with those whose emotional and behavioural difficulties block their progress. Together, these groups often make up the majority identified as having SEN. The challenge for teachers is to cover the individual needs of basic skills in reading, spelling, handwriting and mathematics, and appropriate learning behaviour, while at the same time giving full access to a broad, balanced curriculum. The Primary Strategy was launched in May 2003. Its aims were to empower primary schools to take control of their curriculum and be more innovative. The Literacy and Numeracy Strategies are now embedded as part of the Primary Strategy.

The Primary Strategy encourages schools to use the freedoms they already have to suit their pupils and the context in which they work.

(Standards website: www.standards.dfes.gov.uk)

It is in the area of classroom management strategies and relationships that teachers require most help. A tension is created by the need to meet individual needs, while increasing the overall standards in literacy and numeracy. Effective use of group work, particularly when other adults are available for support, seems one solution; increasing pupils' independence through self-organised learning, is another.

Developing thinking and social skills

There are a number of published schemes to help children develop their problem-solving and thinking skills. Teachers help children to listen to each other, take turns in speaking and conduct the dialogue so that children learn to follow a line of argument and express their own ideas. When used in this way these programmes improve speaking and listening, higher order reading skills, as well as moral awareness. The most useful feature of all these programmes seems to be the awareness gained of metacognition, that is, the ability to reflect on one's own thinking processes (see Source List 1b).

Disaffected pupils

Circular 10/99 outlines legal procedures and good practice for managing pupils with very difficult behaviour, especially those at risk of exclusion. For pupils who do not respond to the school's actions and may need longer-term interventions, a Pastoral Support Programme (PSP) should be set up with external services. The advice is that PSPs should not be used for pupils with IEPs or statements for SEN. This circular points out that difficult behaviour may be the result of unmet special needs, thus early identification and suitable support are a priority for such pupils. The circular also points out that 'looked after' children may be particularly vulnerable. It is suggested that it is good practice that a named teacher should take responsibility for the coordination with carers and Social Services. Social and Emotional Aspects of Learning (SEAL) is a curriculum resource to help primary schools develop children's social, emotional and behavioural skills. It was developed in over 500 primary schools and is now to be extended to secondary schools (see www.standards. dfes.gov.uk/primary/publications/benda/seal/).

SENCos and teachers can work together to:

* Develop a positive learning culture which builds a strong learning community.
* Find ways of improving classroom management and organisation, including effective use of support staff and productive group work. Offer each other support, particularly with challenging pupil behaviour.
* Maximise peer group support through well resourced group activities: teaching pupils strategies of working collaboratively and solving problems together.
* Maximise use of any available adult help to reduce group size for key activities requiring mediated learning or specific teaching of skills.
* Aim to improve pupils' self-esteem and motivation to learn, and increasing their autonomy and by celebrating success.
* Improve lesson planning, using individual assessment information and specialist skills to contribute to curriculum differentiation.
* Teach thinking and study skills and apply these to the handling of information needed for other subject areas.
* Encourage use of appropriate information technology; taped books, computer programmes and alternative ways of recording work.
* Continue to work closely with parents and carers, involving them in target-setting and giving them a role in helping their child.

Assessment arrangement: Key Stages 2 and 3

SENCos need to be up-to-date with current special assessment arrangements for the end of Key Stages 2 and 3, which may change each year. Details are available from the Qualifications and Curriculum Authority. Permission for special arrangements is required by specified dates.

Key Stage 3: 11–14 years

Many of the characteristics of Key Stage 2 continue to apply. New features are the scale of the organisation in secondary schools and the need to work with all curriculum areas and the pastoral system. Communication is therefore the key issue. This begins by communication between phases and dissemination of important information to all staff about the pupils that they will teach. Staff should be given key information in time to plan before mistakes are made at the critical transfer period (see Chapter 8). For the pupil, it is important that as curriculum pressure increases, a sense of achievement can still be maintained.

This means setting up systems so that the dissemination of relevant information about students' needs is given to all staff and influences their curriculum delivery. The majority of targets set with the pupil should be challenging but achievable within normal differentiated curriculum delivery and class management.

The SENCo, or learning support team, should ideally be available to give advice and help staff development across departments on strategies for class management, differentiation by task, resource and support. Another key role will be the organisation of support for pupils with statements, as well as those on the School Action and School Action Plus of the graduated response of the Code of Practice. The support team also can encourage styles of teaching which take into account a variety of learning styles and help pupils develop successful learning strategies. Partnership teaching may be an effective way to share expertise between the learning support staff and others. These options are not possible if all the support comes from teaching assistants.

Attention should also be paid to the effects on pupils' motivation of particular organisational features, such as banding and streaming. In some schools pupils are withdrawn for extra help in literacy and while this may be valuable, it is important to keep in mind the rights of all pupils to take full part in the life of the school.

Structures for meetings, within and between departments, will need to be worked out as part of whole-school policy. Subject departments could, for example, have a link teacher for SEN, who meets with the SENCo on a regular basis. Links to the pastoral system are vital; so that learning support teachers and teaching assistants, form tutors and heads of year communicate important information about students' needs and actions taken. Examples of good practice can be found in the companion book to this one, Cowne (2003) *Developing Inclusive Practice*. Target-setting for all pupils can be linked to systems of academic tutoring aimed at raising achievement for all.

Key issues for the Learning Support Department

- Supporting teachers to differentiate the curriculum appropriately for all pupils.
- Providing access to specialist knowledge in assessment strategies and planning for those with significant LDD.
- Collecting information from each department about an individual pupil's progress and sharing relevant information with colleagues.
- For those with IEPs, designing these so that targets are challenging and achievable and self-esteem enhanced. Reviewing these frequently.
- Dissemination of SEN information amongst relevant staff and departments, including special assessment arrangements at end of KS3.

- Encouraging the teaching of study skills and checking on readability of texts and worksheets.
- Informing senior management of time and resources needed between and among pupils with SEN – (a key issue in the SEN policy).
- Monitoring the effects of organisational features, such as setting, on pupil motivation and disaffection.
- Continuing to work closely with parents, keeping them informed and listening to problems. Some of these arise round homework. This can be difficult for SEN pupils. The SENCo may need to mediate between subject teacher and pupil to make homework demands reasonable for the family and pupil.
- Ensuring that students have access to careers guidance, working in partnership with career staff or services at the end of KS3.
- Being aware of those students who will need special exam access so that this can be built into support work at KS4.

Key Stage 4: 14–16

At Key Stage 4 the issue about differentiation or modification changes to one about choice of courses and subjects. SENCos have an important role to play within the school's decision-making about what courses should be on offer. With their knowledge of student perspectives gained, knowledge of the young person at KS3, and by working with careers consultants and parents, they will know much about the aspirations and capabilities of SEN students. This knowledge can influence the school's policy and planning in how option choices are put together. Schools are now encouraged to consider more flexibility for some of their older pupils who might be more motivated by vocational courses, including work placements. Up to 15 per cent of the existing curriculum time could be available for those pupils who meet the criteria for such courses.

Much of this requires whole-school planning and is, as QCA suggests, for school staff, governors and parents to discuss in order to determine the purposes, principles and possibilities surrounding KS4 choices. The SENCo has a vital role in bringing the SEN perspective to these important discussions. A full discussion of all that is on offer at KS4 lies outside the scope of this book. QCA regularly publishes documents on KS4 and SENCos need to keep up to date with the current situation, which is changing rapidly at present.

The revised curriculum also gives particular flexibility at KS4 to attend school part-time. It is now possible for disaffected youngsters in KS4 to be placed in an alternative programme which aims to give them skills related to work and the adult world and to build their confidence and self-esteem. But it is very important that students with special needs leave school with qualifications and certificates that will help them get employment. This means that the opportunities at KS4 must be relevant to the pupils, but also valued by others such as parents, further education providers and employers.

The revised National Curriculum now requires schools to teach citizenship. The personal and social health education (PHSE) programme will also help schools to develop cross-curricular skills and vocational courses. Circular 10/99 requires a Pastoral Support Programme (PSP) to be put in place for disaffected pupils at risk of exclusion. Liaison with Learning Support is essential, as is partnership with parents or carers. Certain students may move to Pupil Referral Units as part of this programme, others may have a planned move to another school, or to a further education college. In all cases liaison between pastoral teams and the learning support department is essential.

Access arrangements at Key Stage 4

Access arrangements for Key Stage assessments and GCSE include a range of provisions. These include a:

- person to transcribe questions
- scribe
- prompter
- communicator
- transcripts for illegible texts
- rest period.

There are resource implications for schools in supplying these. Information is available from the Joint Council for Qualifications (JCQ) at www.jcq.org.uk.

Schools must present information about students requiring access arrangements on the relevant form for each examination board or type of externally assessed qualification. Most accrediting boards ask for a report from the EP or specialist teacher. Each course has guidance notes so it will be necessary to be familiar with those boards chosen by the school. This may well be a cross-curricular issue and will require coordination. Subject staff will need to know about the types of arrangement possible and about student needs. Special arrangements might include use of a reader or a computer. The student must be used to the processes chosen. This means plans for special arrangements must be in place well before the exam period. It is likely that the SENCo will have an important role in the coordination of paperwork for the students in question.

Further Education

Colleges of FE have learning support departments, employing teachers or TAs to support individual students. The equivalent of the SENCo is the learning support manager. At the FE stage it is essential to pay attention to the young person's viewpoint, remembering that some students may have had poor experiences of support in school. It will be an important part of the entry procedures to negotiate a package of support that the student is comfortable with.

The key roles and issues for the learning support department at both KS4 and FE would seem to be:

- Early counselling and target-setting in partnership with both students and parents about programmes of study choices. This should be based on a range of evidence, including baseline scores, SATs, teacher observations and finding ways to demonstrate pupils' strengths by choosing suitable accredited courses and using other Records of Achievement.
- Inviting a college learning support tutor to the student's final review at school to discuss the support available at college. This can help reassure both student and parent and so ease transition.
- Helping students to self-regulate and monitor their own progress and helping colleagues to recognise the students' strengths and not to emphasise weaknesses.
- Provision of assessment information to accrediting bodies about students who may be entitled to access arrangements in exams, such as additional time, use of information and communications technology, and a reader or an amanuensis.
- Helping colleagues understand and support the access arrangements for exams that may be available and needed for SEN students. It is important to pass on this information to FE to establish history of need and provision.
- Careful planning and discussion of students' work experience placements to ensure inclusion of their personal needs, interests and strengths, which will have a direct influence on their confidence and self-esteem. Work placements which are integral parts of some courses, must be included when considering accessibility and the making of reasonable adjustments.
- The consolidation of cross-curricular links through key skills as described in the revised National Curriculum.
- Providing information to students and their parents or carers on public accreditation, which is realistic and flexible and may include combined programmes of GCSE,

GNVQs, Award Scheme Development Accreditation Network (ASDAN), and other accredited pathways.
- Planning internal school accreditation through Records of Achievement, internal certification and the recognition and celebration of achievement.
- The offer of option support sessions which allow students to review and reinforce Programmes of Study; receive individual and small group support for coursework and general organisation; revision of basic skills, study skills and thinking skills.
- Providing opportunities to link review sessions directly with realistic personal targets and expectations for further accreditation or careers experience.

(Adapted from Cowne and Murphy 2000)

The last two chapters have looked at both theoretical and practical issues related to the delivery of the whole curriculum. The SENCos role in relation to helping colleagues with aspects of teaching and learning is to understand what potential barriers there might be for those with significant learning difficulties and disabilities (LDD). This requires careful observation and assessment, not only of the individual pupils strategies in learning, but also of the classroom environment in which they function. Their aim will be to equip all teachers with a range of appropriate strategies to meet the majority of needs. The pupil themselves will be able to give feedback to teachers as to what helps them and what further support or change is needed. The next two chapters discuss aspects of supporting teaching and learning through the use of additional adults, and through advice from a range of outside agencies.

CHAPTER 6

Managing Effective Support

In recent years, the management of support systems has become a central role for SENCos or senior staff in most schools. Many kinds of additional staff have been funded by the LA or the school to support pupils with SEN. Most pupils with statements for SEN will have been allocated such support and this is often provided by Teaching Assistants (TAs), previously known as Learning Support Assistants (LSAs). The SENCo's role in relation to the coordination and management of support is therefore likely to be significant.

It could include the need to:

- hire, induct and manage support teams – in conjunction with the senior management team;
- provide clear job descriptions for TAs, including Higher Level Teaching Assistants (HLTAs);
- establish the support needs of pupils and colleagues;
- arrange support timetables;
- monitor support in relation to pupil progress;
- arrange liaison time for support teams and subject teachers, including liaison time with the SENCo themselves;
- provide support personally to pupils or staff;
- organise staff development for support teams; induction and continuing professional development (CPD);
- build links with outside support services and agencies and liaise with them to ensure good partnership can occur;
- support individual parents through interviews and case conferences;
- keep the senior management team and governors informed of support issues and resource implications.

This description may seem daunting, but is based on observation of the work of many SENCos. It becomes clear that in large schools, or those with many support staff, the management of support requires time and expertise if it is to be carried out effectively.

Health and safety issues

The health and safety of children and support staff should be carefully thought out as part of school policy. As it is likely that in many schools SENCos will have responsibility for managing TAs, this is an aspect they should address when employing, training and monitoring staff. When a child with a statement is due to arrive and an assistant is hired, the health and safety procedures for the child must be planned. If necessary, professionals from the health service should advise on matters such as lifting, toileting or administering therapies. Support staff may need training to use specialist equipment. Administering medication must follow strictly agreed procedures, with permission from parents. TAs should not normally be left in sole charge of children – if out of the classroom, they must know who is available to help and where this person can be found. Restraint training and procedures should also be covered where applicable, usually under LA procedural advice. Risk assessment should be carried out for all relevant activities (government advice available DfES/DoH (2002)).

Providing and monitoring support

Who provides support?

The range of people who might be found working alongside a class teacher may include: TAs working with statemented children, other TAs employed by the school, learning mentors, therapists, support teachers – either those who are part of the school staff or peripatetic teachers/advisers from an LA service, special school teachers working in an outreach capacity, and volunteers or parents. Schools can now appoint HLTAs. This status is awarded by the Teacher Development Agency (TDA) to staff who have undertaken additional training. HLTAs will have more demanding roles often managing other adults or carrying out specialist work under supervision of a teacher. Deployment of HLTAs will require appropriate job descriptions and suitable timetables. Visiting teachers may offer advice to TAs about individuals or groups.

The SENCo's role as a support teacher

Many SENCos work as support teachers themselves for part of the week. This may be for a few lesson periods, or even a whole timetable that they can organise themselves. SENCos are very experienced teachers and can have much to offer by way of help to pupils and their teachers. A secondary SENCo wrote that the further you go away from the classroom the harder it is to give valid advice, so working part of the week with a 'hands-on experience', keeps you up-to-date with materials and techniques and lends credibility when giving advice to colleagues. However, if SENCos choose to deliver support for too much of the time this could shorten the time for organisational and management work.

SENCo's role in monitoring support

It is possible therefore that there may well be one or more additional adults working in many classrooms. Pupils may also meet several support personnel across a week. Because of the potential complexity of support it is essential that there is a dedicated support policy which establishes some basic principles. Proper record keeping of visits and activities is also essential. It is usually the SENCo's responsibility to monitor overall provision and evaluate its effectiveness. Provision mapping can be a useful tool to track how the school's resources are being used; by recording details of the range of support given to children with SEN in each of the year groups. It assists in costing and could reduce the bureaucracy of writing too many IEPs. Using this approach can also be linked to the 'waves of support' concept of the expanding National Literacy Strategy. Gross and White (2003) describe this approach in more detail (see Chapter 3 and Activity 4).

Types of support

Support to individuals

Part of the strategy to meet individual targets may be to offer additional support from an adult who works alongside the child in class. Their role is to help the pupil be as independent a learner as possible. They will check that instructions have been understood, keep the pupil on task by encouragement and praise, as well as adding additional teaching points. This type of support is often given by TAs and is particularly productive for younger pupils. However, there are dangers in seeing each TA as being attached to one child. This can produce dependency in both the child and the adult. Too many adults in a classroom can be an ineffectual use of resources. Examples in Gerschel (2005).

Support in groups

Adult support is most often given to small groups, even when the target child is the one for whom it was originally allocated. Pupils need time and space to attempt tasks, make and learn from mistakes and develop autonomy. An over-protective type of support will suppress independence. TAs are often given responsibility for teaching groups, but this should be under the supervision of a teacher, who plans the content and delivery of the curriculum and monitors pupil progress. Sometimes, for very short periods, this extra teaching takes place outside the classroom. Sessions must be carefully planned to back up what is happening in class, and flexible timetabling will be needed so that pupils do not lose their curriculum entitlement. Small group work within class may be just as effective, although this depends on features of classroom organisation and space. In some rooms finding space for extra adults is a problem. For certain activities, especially those requiring careful listening, the class environment is too noisy. In other cases the group activity itself will be too disruptive to the rest of the class.

There have been arguments that any form of support that does not take place within the classroom is against inclusive principles, resulting in a form of internal exclusion for certain pupils. This is too simplistic, as individual timetables can be carefully planned to be flexible, and good liaison can help offset missed curricular activities. SENCos should be wary however of too much teaching outside the classroom and must ensure appropriate supervision and monitoring of support. There is also concern about the effects of withdrawal on the pupil's self-image. Younger pupils rarely mind being taken out in a group because their need for extra attention may be greater. With older pupils, it may be best to negotiate and then let them choose what sort of support they would like. Often a 'clinic' approach for such difficulties as spelling and reading can result in self-referral. This is effective for older pupils, especially when they are preparing coursework. The Ofsted (1996) report found that withdrawal sessions were particularly effective in secondary schools in raising pupil standards.

Whatever individual or group support is available, it cannot compensate for a poorly differentiated curriculum. If the focus is solely on the child and not the curriculum and classroom content, this form of support may fail. The location for support need not be problematic, as long as it provides this access and insures progress. The task of the SENCo is to keep inclusive principles at the forefront of everyone's mind when planning the curriculum schemes of work, lesson plans and support timetables.

Extra resourced provision

Sometimes schools are set up as resource centres where pupils with similar needs can be helped by extra support staff. In such provision, sometimes known as a unit, a group of pupils with similar disabilities is taught by a specialist teacher with TA support. Most frequently such units are for those with physical or sensory difficulties or language and communication difficulties. The Ofsted report (2006) found that mainstream schools with extra resourced provision were particularly successful in achieving high outcomes for pupils with LDDs – academically, socially and personally. Pupils spend varying amounts of time in mainstream classes, often supported by TAs. Pupils who have experienced different types of provision often report a strong preference for special schools or units. This is because being the only child who has a certain disability, such as a hearing impairment, can be an isolating experience (MacConville *et al.* 2007).

However, due to parental choice for the neighbourhood school, or LA inclusion policy and priorities, children with a variety of LDD are found in many mainstream schools. Children with many types of LDD are often given TA support, sometimes monitored by specialists from the health service or advisory teachers from either inside or outside the school. TAs often become skilled interpreters of the pupils' wishes and advocates for pupils (see Appendix 6 for details).

Supporting curriculum differentiation/modification

This view of support can be seen as an additional means of ensuring that the curriculum is accessible to a wider range of pupils with learning difficulties. It often takes the form of collaborative partnerships where two teachers or a team of adults plan and deliver aspects of the subject and where good use of group work is possible. It requires excellent joint planning to use the skills and knowledge of those involved. The SENCo may act in the role of support teacher as a means of helping develop good practice.

TAs can support the curriculum too, not by planning whole lessons, but by sharing ideas of how to follow up a theme or produce a resource. Gerschel (2005) found that TAs frequently complain of being asked to modify and interpret teaching in a lesson, often without prior notice of what is being taught. Innovative ideas can be generated as long as curriculum goals have been made clear to them *in advance* of the lesson delivery. Prerequisite skills and concepts can be rehearsed with pupils prior to a lesson and this is often a very useful form of support. Specialist materials can also be produced by TAs under instruction. Allowing the full potential of the support team will benefit all of the children in the class, but will require joint planning and training, including the understanding of the importance of role definition.

The Ofsted report (2006) found that pupils in mainstream schools, where support from TAs was the main provision, were less likely to make academic progress than those who had access to specialist teachers in these schools. They also say that although TAs provide valuable support and undertake difficult roles, they should not be a substitute for focused highly skilled teaching. This would seem to indicate that working with TAs produces most progress when teachers with specialist knowledge lead the planning.

Liaison time

Hart (1991) states that successful collaborative partnerships are made, not born, and are a product of continual careful negotiation. The classroom context is part of the experience that affects children's individual responses to learning. These are a product of the conditioning that goes on in classrooms. Hart argues that differentiating the curriculum to meet individual needs is also about understanding these classroom processes. She says,

> What we call individual differences are thus not objective descriptions of individual qualities and characteristics which exist independently of school and classroom contexts and the interpretative frameworks of teachers. They are products of school and classroom processes, not simply a natural reflection of inherent differences in children.
>
> (Hart 1995: 38)

Working together, adults can help each other make sense of the complexity of the classroom environment. Successful teams will take time to analyse the various elements of classroom interactions and evaluate how support can best contribute to solving the various problems that arise. However, time is scarce and rarely of sufficient quality to allow this to happen. Liaison time is often not seen as a priority by senior management, but it has certainly been seen as a key factor by Ofsted (1996).

SENCos should explain to senior managers that classroom teams need time to work out their respective roles and responsibilities and for regular planning and feedback on pupil's progress. It will therefore be an important part of the SENCo's role to fight for such time to be available for classroom teams to work together on some regular basis. Without liaison time, what could be the most effective way to support the curriculum and the child with LDD is ineffective and this considerable additional resource could thus be wasted.

Training support personnel

Balshaw (1999) gives useful guidance on the training needs of TAs. She lists some principles which should be addressed when planning a training programme. These include:

- establishing clear roles and responsibilities; this includes relationships to pupils, parents and teachers;
- gaining clear understanding of the communication systems of school and class;
- developing consistency of approaches towards positive provision;
- establishing ground rules for each team – valuing the assistants' work and not using them as 'dogsbodies';
- offering support for personal and professional skills development.

To which I would add:

- understanding National Curriculum principles and assessment procedures in outline;
- learning principles about teaching reading, writing and mathematics;
- outlining key issues about managing behaviour;
- different types of disabilities and learning difficulties;
- using IT to support learning;
- helping enhance self-esteem.

Fox (2003), Lorenz (1998) and Balshaw (1999) all emphasise the need to train TAs and teachers together so that policies and practices for support move forward in a coherent manner. Misunderstandings over roles and responsibilities are much more easily sorted out by joint training. Balshaw (1999) gives examples of staff development exercises which will aid such joint training enterprises. Fox (2003) contains useful chapters for both TAs and class teachers, explaining their work together. TDA (2006) has established a high quality programme of training materials. Gerschel (2005) states that National Occupational Standards have now been developed and a range of professional qualifications for support staff has emerged from NVQs to Foundation Degrees (LSC 2004).

The SENCo's role in managing support

The SENCo's role is to coordinate the SEN work in the school. Part of this will be to encourage other teachers to differentiate the curriculum and organise the classroom, so that the majority of needs can be met from within the normal resources of the school. Often best practice for those with additional needs produces better provision for all pupils. To do this will mean that:

- *SENCos must keep an overview of what is happening to support staff in their school.* This means setting up a meeting system where the groups of TAs can voice concerns, sort out problems about children or staff and generally feel supported themselves. Monitoring the success of support and its relationship to pupil progress is a vital role for SENCos.

For effective management there should be:

> a viable organisational structure within the school with clearly defined roles and responsibilities for TAs, their managers, including the SENCo and the teaching staff with whom they work and active support training and direction for schools from the LA.
>
> (Gerschel 2005: 70)

TAs, like other staff, are entitled to regular reviews of their performance, and SENCos may find themselves taking on this role. It requires observation of TAs at work and thoughtful discussion of how TAs' strengths can be used most effectively and areas for improvement supported.

- *SENCos will need to provide support to families.* SENCos spend a great deal of time in this activity and it may be a most effective way to support the child. Talking to parents of children with difficulties, finding out their concerns and worries and entering into agreements over goals, are all ways of supporting parents and through this, their children. Listening to parents and being aware of their anxieties is an important aspect of the SENCo's consultative role, which is explored further in Chapter 10.
- *The SENCo will be needed most for advice in assessing and planning for those with more intractable and persistent needs.* This may require them to teach in order to get to know the pupil in his/her environment. SENCos also need to know who may be called in to advise from local services beyond the school (see Chapter 7).

Support for the SENCo

For an effective SEN policy to work the SENCo needs support from senior management. SENCos should work to a deputy head or be part of the Senior Leadership Team (SLT). There are many decisions that need to be shared and communication is vital between the SENCo and management.

Many LAs hold SENCo network meetings on at least a termly basis. These meetings serve to support the work of the SENCo and to share ideas across the district. If this is not happening, perhaps a cluster of schools could get together to arrange meetings. They might make themselves into a branch of a national organisation such as NASEN (National Association of Special Educational Needs) and use this to organise in-service training (see Source List 1b). Such networks of support give everyone opportunities to hear what others do, to problem-solve and to agree on local procedures and priorities. The SENCo Forum, set up by the National Council for Educational Technology, provides an Internet conference for subscribers and helps SENCos from becoming isolated (see Source List 1b).

Clerical support for SENCos

The Code of Practice (DfES 2001b: 6.10) points out the value of allocating administrative staff time to help the SENCo, thus releasing the SENCo to use his or her expertise more effectively. This would come from funding devolved to schools for SEN. There are now also many commercial software packages to help in the production of IEPs, although it is important to research whether these provide value and meet SENCos needs, as many are expensive.

SENCo training

The SENCo role is continually developing. In some schools SENCos are leaders, managing change as part of the SLT. In others they may be class teachers with little or no time to develop their role. At both ends of this continuum, SENCos need support through training, some of which is on-going. Many LAs offer SENCos regular meetings to discuss common issues and keep up with government legislation and advice. However, SENCos also need access to longer training courses. The National Standards for SENCos, issued by the Teacher Training Agency in 1998, listed key areas of SEN coordination. The following then became key areas for SENCo training:

- strategic direction and development of SEN provision in the school
- teaching and learning
- leading and managing staff
- efficient and effective development of staff and resources.

The NUT survey (2004) asked SENCos what training they had experienced and what was needed. The survey reported constraints in attending training, even where on offer, were due to budget cuts and lack of time. This report identified a need for external national training. Although some good quality training has been available through partnerships between some LAs and IHEs, schools have found it difficult to release the SENCo to attend. New draft legislation, under consultation at the beginning of 2008, proposes that in future SENCos must be qualified teachers or taking steps to meet the requirements. The recommendation that all SENCos should be part of the SLT has not been incorporated into the statutory regulation, although it will be strongly advised where possible. House of Commons Select Committee report (2006) indicated that in future all SENCos should be offered access to national training schemes. The TDA has carried out consultations on how a national scheme for accrediting newly appointed SENCos might operate. The DCSF however, say that it is not possible to introduce this mandatory training requirement until further development and consultation is carried out.

From the author's experience of SENCo training for over two decades, the following learning outcomes for SENCo courses are recommended. At the end of such a course SENCos should be able to show knowledge and understanding of:

- personal learning and ability to reflect on their practice with reference to key issues and concepts of inclusion and disability awareness;
- the emerging roles of the SENCo with reference to recent, relevant documents and developments in schools;
- the role of the SENCo in relation to leading and managing others while working within a whole-school approach to provision for children/young people with a range of LDD;
- a range of assessment models and strategies, including observation and pupil interviews, which apply to Assessment for Learning, and of various methods of recording and tracking progress for pupils with SEN;
- the issues related to working collaboratively with class/subject teachers and support staff to enhance inclusive classroom practice in learning and teaching;
- working within the cross-agency Every Child Matters agenda relevant to their own LA.

Reviewing support policies

This chapter has explored types of support and considered how to make support more effective. Several points to remember emerge for SENCos. SENCos have a role in explaining the importance of these issues to the SLT and governors. If not addressed, valuable resources may be wasted or not used efficiently for the benefit of the pupils. These are:

- policies need to include information about how support will be monitored to give evidence of pupil progress and of listening to pupil views;

- time for liaison and training must be allocated by senior management and governors as part of the school's SEN Policy. The Ofsted report (1996) *Promoting high achievement for pupils with SEN* stated that, 'the most influential factor on the effectiveness of in-class support is the quality of joint planning of the work between class/subject teacher and the support teacher;
- on induction, support staff should have job descriptions and guidance notes, and preferably the opportunity to shadow an experienced TA for two or three days. They also need a line manager, who is often the SENCo, with whom regular meetings are possible;
- SENCos also need to monitor their own time management and balance the various aspects of management of support, teaching children, seeing parents/carers and training adults who support children;
- SENCos themselves need access to support groups and national good quality training courses.

Cowne (2003) gives examples of how SENCos in training reviewed support policies as part of their course work. Activity 5 may be used as an audit to monitor the support policy. It can be adapted to cover other aspects of support work particular to your school.

CHAPTER 7

Multi-professional Networks

This chapter looks at the partnership with bodies beyond the school and how this links to the school's SEN policy and practice as laid out in the Code of Practice (2001) (Regulation 3 (1), Schedule 1, Section 3) (see Appendix 2b).

> Such services include specialist teachers of pupils with hearing, visual, and speech and language impairments, teachers providing more general learning and behaviour support services, counsellors, educational psychologists, and advisers or teachers with knowledge of information technology for children with special educational needs. Curriculum support and advisory services can also be a resource for advice on specific subject-related teaching techniques and strategies and curriculum materials.
>
> (Code of Practice, DfES 2001b: 10.7)

Since 2000, LEAs have been delegating funding for most services to schools. At the same time, government has indicated a new role for special schools in delivering outreach services. However, the 2005 Ofsted report found that too little guidance had been given as to how outreach services should be delivered and fit into local provision. They also stated that lack of long-term funding had undermined their ability to plan strategically.

Ofsted (2006) found that 'special schools had a particular strength in carefully matching the skills and interest of staff to the needs of groups of pupils, but teachers in mainstream schools had a better knowledge of individual subjects in the National Curriculum'. There is therefore scope for further sharing of expertise and collaborative arrangements (see Tutt 2007a for case studies).

Local Authority (LA) duties

The LA still has a duty under the Code of Practice to inform schools of education services that are available and how these should be accessed and funded. LAs must also ascertain the demand for the SEN services from schools. As a response to the Children Act (2004) and *Every Child Matters: Change for Children*, former LEAs are now called LAs (Local Authorities) and under a Director of Children's Services. Tutt says, 'This means the main services used by families: education, health and social care will be working more closely together and be more readily accessible' (Tutt 2007a: 7).

Due to delegation of funding many support services have been lost. A small service funded by the LA could target support where it was required. When these funds were delegated, in some cases, schools received too little money to buy in the necessary support, while other schools who did not have the need used money for other purposes. Ofsted (2005) found that service delivery is too variable across the country:

> The delegation of funding for support services had a negative effect on the provision for some pupils with SEN. It diminished the capacity of many LEAs to monitor the progress of pupils with SEN and reduced the range and quantity of specialist staff available to provide advice and support.
>
> (Ofsted 2005: 3)

The following services however usually remain centrally funded by LAs.

Educational Psychological Services (EPS)

Each LA in England and Wales has an Educational Psychological Service (EPS). Educational psychologists from the EPS may work a 'patch' system, looking after a cluster of schools on a regular basis, or be part of a multi-disciplinary area team under Children's Services. They form an important resource for a school, especially when they work there on a regular basis. Their role has been linked to providing assessment and advice for the statementing procedure, although this role is reducing. They can be invaluable when giving advice to teachers about pupil behaviour or other pupils causing concern. EPs often run projects to develop new strategies or techniques and support staff development. Increasingly, the EPs role is to advise schools on interventions for Wave 3 Literacy Strategy and to help develop provision management.

Education Welfare Service (sometimes called Education Social Workers) (EWS)

Education Welfare Officers (EWOs) are employed by the LA to help parents/carers and the LA meet statutory obligations in relation to school attendance. They can play an important role with pupils who also have SEN, in helping liaise between home and school and maintaining communication in cases where attendance is sporadic. There are often underlying reasons for poor attendance which relate to learning or behavioural difficulties. Partnership between SENCos and EWOs can be very productive in sorting out some of these underlying difficulties and easing a pupil back to school. EWOs can provide support and counselling for those children not in school or at risk of exclusion.

Parent partnership services

These are statutory and while most remain part of the LA, they are encouraged to operate independently. Their roles and responsibilities are set out in the Code of Practice (2001: 2). Their purpose is to provide unbiased information and support to parents/carers often in relation to the statementing procedure, but also about other aspects of education.

Behaviour and Education Support Teams (BEST)

These are multi-agency teams of 4-5 members who focus on pupils whose attendance and/or behaviour is causing a problem. Personnel are likely to include an EP, EWO, Behaviour Support Staff and Social Workers, although others from the health service may be included.

Pupil Referral Units (PRUs)

These units were set up under the 1996 Education Act to offer local provision for pupils who were out of school, usually through exclusion. Many such pupils have

BESD, some with statements. Some PRUs are linked to Behavioural Support Services which may be run as outreach from a special school. Pupils can be dually registered at a PRU and a school.

Child health services

Many District Health Authorities do not overlap geographically with LAs. There may therefore be more than one health authority with which an LA must communicate. The SENCo needs to know the relevant authority for their school. A school's first point of contact will be through the local school health service, whose professionals include speech and language therapists, occupational therapists and physiotherapists, community paediatricians, doctors and the school nurse. Local hospitals will also have a paediatric service in which physiotherapists and occupational therapists will work. Just how much hospital services can work with schools varies enormously from district to district. Schools may consult health services with the parent/carer's consent when wishing to check whether there is a medical condition which may be contributing to a child's difficulty in school.

If necessary, and with informed consent and involvement of the child's parents/carers, a special medical examination can be requested. It is wise to check that hearing and vision, for example, have been examined. The school health service will have records of school-aged children, especially if there are known special needs, which can be accessed as necessary.

Pupils on regular medication for conditions such as asthma, diabetes or epilepsy do not have special educational needs as such, but may miss some schooling. Certain pupils may have aids and appliances which need to be maintained by a clinical technician; an obvious example being hearing aids. Children with more severe disabilities will have been identified in early childhood by the Health Authority and the LA will have been notified. GPs, however, may be less aware of the Code of Practice. Child community health is the best source of information for schools. As the Common Assessment Framework (CAF) is rolled out into practice, it will be used by all practitioners across services to assess additional needs and services.

Child and Adolescent Mental Health Services (CAMHS)

Some children and young people identified as having SEN may benefit from referral to CAMHS – specialists for assessment and interventions for mental health problems. CAMHS can also provide support and consultation to family members, carers and workers from health, social care, educational and voluntary agencies (Code of Practice, DfES 2001b: 10.28). Permission from parents and carers must be sought to enable CAMHS to share information with schools.

Social services

Social service departments should ensure that all schools in their area know the name of and how to contact the designated social services officer who has responsibility for pupils with SEN. Every child who is 'looked after' by the local authority must have a care plan which sets out their long-term objectives. This will incorporate the Personal Education Plan, giving any SEN arrangements (Code of Practice, DfES 2001b: 10.37).

Not all such children will have SEN, so may not be the responsibility of the SENCo. Liaison within school between SEN and pastoral systems will be important in these cases. The SEN policy needs to set out clearly the arrangements for working in partnership with social services and who on the school staff has responsibility for liaison, information collection and dissemination, and individual planning which links to IEPs and Personal Education Plans. Again, the CAF should help improve collaboration in future.

The Connexions service

> Connexions is a multi-agency service, which provides information, advice and guidance to young people, along with access to personal development opportunities. It aims to remove barriers to learning and progression, and ensure young people make a smooth transition to adulthood and working life. Connexions is currently going through a process of transition. By April 2008, the funding that currently goes directly to the 47 Connexions partnerships will go to the 150 local authority areas.
>
> *(Every Child Matters: Change for Children*, DfES 2004a)

The service is delivered through a network of personal advisors linking in with specialist support services. The service will give greater priority to those young people at greatest risk (see also Chapter 8).

Voluntary organisations

Many disability groups have charities which concentrate on one impairment. The best known are organisations such as the Royal National Institute for the Blind (RNIB), Royal National Institute for the Deaf (RNID), Invalid Children's Aid Nationwide (ICAN) and SCOPE (formally the Spastics Society) (see Source List 2). Some of these have set up specialist schools and training for specialist teachers. However, all are involved in providing training and consultancy services. There are large numbers of smaller groups specialising in a wide range of disabilities. One of the key roles of voluntary organisations is to put parents/carers in touch with others in the same situation as themselves. This, combined with factual information about the disability, is the most important way voluntary organisations can be used. There are also local generic groups supporting parents/carers and children with all types of SEN. Local addresses should be available from Educational Psychological Services (EPS) or the Education Officer for SEN. Parent Partnership Officers will also have contacts. SENCos need to build up an information folder of local and national organisations, which include named contacts with telephone numbers.

> The DfES sponsors a network of eleven SEN Regional Partnerships. These bring together groups of local authorities and local health, social services, voluntary and private sector partners. The overall aim of the network is to secure greater consistency in the quality of the response to pupils with similar special educational needs.
>
> (Code of Practice, DfES 2001b: 10.39)

The SENCo's role in working within the multi-professional network

One of the SENCo's key roles is getting to know and working with the various support services and agencies that are available locally. There should be a file in the school giving basic information, including names and contact numbers, for all the agencies and services and how referrals can be made. It may be useful to include the addresses and contacts of special schools as they too have expertise and may be able to offer advice which is increasingly a coordinated outreach service. The first task for a new SENCo is to see whether the school has this directory of services or the equivalent. Once the names and telephone numbers are known, the next step is to get to know the relevant members of the services. These could be the SEN Advisor; the Assistant Education Officer (Special); the Educational Psychologist; the teachers in support services; the community health centre personnel; doctor and school nurse. These will give access to a range of additional professionals, such as therapists. Added to this, there is a need to be aware of the voluntary organisations that have national networks and local branches or representatives. All of these services, agencies and organisations will work with parents/carers, as will the school. The Code of Practice (DfES 2001b) strongly suggests that SENCos should have access to a telephone to fulfil duties related to networking with others.

The SENCo often plays a co-coordinating role for parents/carers by putting them in touch with the multi-professional network, or by collating information from the various agencies who may work with the child and family. All parents/carers have a key role to play with their children, especially those with SEN. Parents/carers vary, from 'key workers' who have for years coordinated information about their child, to parents/carers who lack confidence and need encouragement to share information and make decisions with the school. The SENCo also has a key role in leading other staff and ensuring that continuing professional development opportunities are appropriate and regard the various aspects of SEN, including working in partnership with those beyond the school.

Getting to know key workers from health/social services

Because the focus of work of health or social service personnel is different from that of the school, they will have different priorities, although with the development of the Children's Service, this may change. One way to overcome potential professional barriers is to get to know the individual worker on an informal basis outside of the case conference or meeting situation. Inviting professionals to school staff meetings to explain their roles and share ideas with teachers and TAs can be very helpful. Joint working practices can then be decided and then, when there is a problem to be solved, this joint understanding will lead to better results. The school nurse, for example, is a resource that is undervalued in many schools. Therapists and other health and social work professionals may also be persuaded to visit schools on a one-off basis as part of an awareness training session.

The Common Assessment Framework (CAF)

The CAF is a key aspect of the *Every Child Matters: Change for Children* programme aiming at transforming services for children with additional needs. The CAF is a standardised approach to assessment and decision-making. It is intended that it will be used by all practitioners from education, health, social services etc. in partnership with the child and family. It is intended to be a simple holistic process of assessment of a child's needs and strengths. Its use aims to improve integrated working by promoting coordinated service provision. Recent DfES research by Brandon *et al.* (2006) evaluated pilot schemes and although the use of CAF was in its early stages, there are lessons to be learnt from their findings.

Aims of CAF

The CAF considers three 'domains':

- How well a child is developing, including their health and progress in learning
- How well parents/carers are able to support their child's development and respond appropriately to any needs
- The impact of wider family and environmental elements on a child's development and on the capacity of their parents and carers.

(Brandon *et al.* 2006: 22)

CAF and schools

Some schools are developing multi-agency centres, sometimes as part of the extended services through schools. Teachers may have too little time to complete CAFs, however, other school-based staff such as learning mentors and TAs may be best placed to carry out the assessment. Attention must, however, be paid to the subsequent workload issues.

Some learning support services and psychologists may have a range of specialists in their teams. Referrals to the service may initially be through the regular key worker, but that person will often know someone else who can help in special cases.

EPs usually have good contacts with health and social services and may be the first contact for many referrals. On the other hand, some specialist services, e.g. hearing and vision, prefer direct contact. The introduction of integrated Children's Services and the CAF should make a common referral process more efficient in future.

From the above it is clear that, as part of their SEN policy, schools need to develop their procedures for referrals and requests to support services and agencies, in conjunction with their own LA's ECM development. Where there are a number of possible choices, decisions need to be made about the best route for support and advice. Over referral to a number of agencies at one time, for the same case, is ineffective and wasteful of scarce resources. Many schools hold a regular half-termly SEN training meeting in order to prioritise referrals in outside agencies. The role of the Lead Professional, when fully developed, should help coordination.

Statement support

In many LAs support for statements has been delegated to schools. When this happens, the school receives a certain sum of money and must purchase or provide support for the pupil in accordance with the statement. They may wish to buy in advice from specialist teachers, either from the LA or, where available, from independent services or those attached to charities. Such service provision will be paid for from delegated funds and must be carefully recorded and monitored as part of the pupil's annual review.

Services working collaboratively with teachers and SENCos

The overwhelming demand from teachers, when getting outside advice and support, is often for strategies to meet the Wave 3 intervention targets, which are manageable within the normal structure of daily teaching. Some services therefore, though excellent for carrying out assessment and 'teasing out' any within-child factors causing a problem, may not directly support teachers or SENCos. An understanding of the curriculum and the social context of the classroom and school are needed if staff are to be fully supported in meeting the needs of more complex individuals. Teachers may need to borrow equipment for a short time to try it out and many will need training about how it should be used. IT can help many pupils with SEN, but knowing which equipment or software to buy and whether it will fit the pupils' needs requires expertise. Over time schools develop this expertise themselves, but it is useful to have specialist teachers who can give advice about matching resources to pupil needs. The SENCo should keep tracks on the extra resources provided or borrowed and be accountable for their efficient use.

Keeping a record of service provision

It is also important in school to keep a record of who has been asked to help for any one child. This should be part of the paperwork attached to the individual records. It is good practice to list outside agency involvement (including dates) and indicate if a report is attached. Communication within the school about referrals is vital, especially when some services are used by the pastoral systems, and other services by the learning support department. There are cases where, for example, a pupil with LDD is excluded and the SENCo was not asked to contribute what is known about the pupil's difficulties. If outside services or agencies are given referrals by a school, the parents or carers must be informed and in the majority of cases, give permission. However, when services support staff rather than the pupils, parental permission would be inappropriate.

Writing effective advice

For schools, the best professional advice is that which helps to contribute to the child's individual planning in a practical way. For pupils with statements, the advice in the

Appendices will have informed the statement writer, who will have then listed the needs and priority objectives for the school to achieve (for statement advice, see Appendix 9). On receipt of such a full statement, targets must then be set by the school, which will be looked at during at the Annual Review. If the report from the professional is full of jargon and results of tests unknown to the school, this is not helpful.

Joint problem-solving sessions

There are a number of puzzling pupils for whom it is not quite clear what is needed. Often the best way to support these pupils most effectively will be to enhance their teacher's own professional skills in the management of the class. If a visiting professional can find time for a joint problem-solving session with a group of staff, they can together elicit the information already known and produce questions which then can be followed up in an assessment. This will give the staff some strategies to try themselves, as well as providing added focus on the type of further information needed and from whom it could be expected. Such sessions make good use of the scarce professional expertise and help teachers to realise they may already have answers to some of their questions. As the Audit Commission states:

> Success of support teams should not always by measured only be pupil progress. Schools may require both direct and indirect support and general guidance. Evaluation should take account of any role in increasing schools' capacities for managing pupils with SEN.
>
> (Audit Commission 1992: 55)

This means services must meet teachers' as well as the child's needs. If a teacher feels supported by knowledge that she or he is doing the right thing and can see the pupil taking a full part in school life and making progress, this will have been a piece of effective support. If, on the other hand, the expert advice has puzzled, confused or de-skilled the teacher, support will not have been so effective.

Parents and carers as part of the multi-professional network

Parents/carers need to know about outside services and agencies and have their various roles explained, especially if there is multi-agency involvement. Again this is best done informally, before the parent/carer has to face a room full of strangers at an annual review or a case conference. Parents/carers themselves will often be the SENCo's best source of information. If the child has been known to the health service since pre-school years, then the parent will know key workers from the community health services or the hospitals who have already worked with the child and provided advice.

In very complex cases the child may be known to up to 30 professionals. So, for such complex disability cases the parent may, in reality, be the key worker for their child; linking the therapies and advice together into an individual plan. Notes will be kept by each service in their files, but it is the parent who has the total picture. In cases where, for example, three therapists require programmes of practice at home, there may not be time for the 'just ten minutes' practice for school as well. School support services cannot focus on the parent's adult needs, but they can support parents/carers to support their children.

Strategic policy planning

One of the elements of the strategic development of policy and practice given in the TTA Standards (1998) document is the liaison with and coordination of the contribution of external agencies. This may include the interpretation of specialist assessment data and its use to inform practice. It is at the stage of School Action Plus that the SENCo's role in working collaboratively with colleagues and support services becomes most important.

This chapter has described in some detail the complexity of working within a multi-professional network. SENCos will need to develop their own style of working which fits the context of their school and LA. What is available will vary from district to district. Internal school organisation also varies enormously. In some schools, heads and senior managers deal with the outside agencies, in others it is the SENCo. Whatever the system, communication will be the key issue if the SENCo is to carry out their role effectively.

CHAPTER 8

Working in Partnership at Transition Periods

The SENCo needs to take a strong lead in helping colleagues to plan both entry and departure from the school for pupils with SEN. These are key points in the pupil's life; good planning, record-keeping and communication can make a great deal of difference to their well-being. There are three critical action times:

- *Entry to school*: planned entry is necessary for children identified in pre-school as having special educational needs or a disability, with or without a statement.
- *Transition between phases or schools*: usually primary/secondary although infant/junior or first/middle possible, as are changes due to moving house.
- *Leaving school*: for college or adult life. This involves the transition plan for pupils with statements but should be planned for all pupils with identified SEN/disability.

All of these may involve working in a multi-disciplinary partnership. School policies should include a section where transfer procedures and the roles and responsibilities related to flow of information are made clear.

Early years and entry to school

Certain children have their special needs identified shortly after birth or before they are two or three years old. Health professionals will often have taken the lead in this identification process and will have informed the LA, who may carry out multi-professional assessments for a statement for those whose needs warrant this.

Education offers some pre-school services, for example, a Portage home visiting service, which works directly with parents using a developmental checklist to identify the next learning step. Services for hearing and vision also make home visits as soon as the disability is identified. Information about local provision for suitable placement for those with disabilities can be obtained from the local Children's Information Services (CIS). Parents should be encouraged to make contact with their local Early Years Development and Child Care Partnership (EYDCP). There are now also programmes to help parents/carers prepare children for nursery school such as Early Start which is a family programme developed by the Basic Skills Agency, based on evidence from the Sure Start groups. It brings together education, health and care services and is aimed at supporting parents of children from birth to three years old where parents or carer live in the most socially and economically disadvantaged communities. Early Start has developed programmes for parents of children about to start nursery schools, focusing on language, literacy and mathematical understanding.

Planning entry to school from this variety of provision requires good liaison from all concerned. Usually some joint planning has taken place with the school SENCo or class teacher, using the knowledge gained by the personnel who will have worked with the child and family before school entry. One of the statutory requirements of the new Early Years curriculum will be to assess every child at the end of the Foundation Stage; in the final term in which the child reaches the age of five. A profile is then completed by a practitioner as a record of achievement. A written summary of progress must then be provided for the parent/carer. For those with SEN, additional assessment may be needed.

Childcare Act 2006

The Act requires Early Years providers to give information about assessments they have carried out to LAs. For those children who attend more than one setting, providers must take account of all available records or discussions with parents/carers from previous settings.

Area SENCos

The government aim is that each LA/EYDCP should fund an area SENCo to support non-maintained early years settings in the ratio of 1:20. The area SENCo supports the setting based SENCo by:

- offering support and advice regarding individual children with additional needs within the Foundation Stage;
- delivering training to Early Years providers;
- supporting transition planning from home to pre-school and then to school;
- establishing effective working links to a range of agencies.

Many LAs also have an under-fives multi-disciplinary panel which can give advice about a child's needs to the receiving school. There are important issues about entry to school for these more vulnerable children. Arrangements need to be flexible and an offer of gradual entry into the full-time experience of school life should be available. Parents have a vital role to play in this planned entry. The Code of Practice (2001), Chapter 4, shows clearly how the graduated response to identifying and assessing those with SEN should be used in Early Years Settings.

This means that some children may have been placed on *Early Years Action* or *Early Years Action Plus* in their early years setting and an IEP may be in place on entry to school. This planning should help to build on what has already been done and help shape a smooth transition to school. It is therefore essential that good use is made of pre-school records when planning to build on existing achievements. Teachers should read and use the Foundation Stage records and other information available from all sources, including information from parents.

Disability Rights Commission Code of Practice (2002)

The DRC Code of Practice (2002b) explains the duties of the responsible body (governors in the case of maintained schools). This Code gives examples of what can be considered as reasonable. As the duties are anticipatory the implication is that admission policies themselves must not be discriminatory. Staff training may also be seen as part of this anticipatory duty. If a child moves to a new district, responsibility for changes to the statement will be transferred to the new LA. The new LA may place a child in a different school from that named on the statement prior to amendment or re-assessment. Parents must be informed within six weeks of transfer when the statement will be reviewed and whether the LA will make a re-assessment (Chapter 8; Code of Practice, DfES 2001b). Part 4 of the statement will always need changing if a child moves to another school in the same LA because of a change of address or a phase change.

Transition from class-to-class

Internal transfer between classes or between infant/junior departments is also important. For the child, having friends matters most, so attention should be paid to friendship groups as well as academic information. Most schools have a new-class visit day in the summer term so that all children will have met their new teacher and have knowledge of where they are going at the start of the autumn term. Children who move home a great deal are the most vulnerable when it comes to transition planning. Schools with mobile populations work on effective procedures for induction, assessment and contact with the previous school, but each school should have clear policies about newcomers who may arrive without records.

It is important that all who teach the child are informed of the child's additional needs. Schools must review the child's progress during the course of the year using normal curriculum and pastoral arrangements, as well as IEPs. Although the Code does not specify this in detail the assumption is that the same good practice applies to pupils who have been placed on *School Action* or *School Action Plus*. Parents should be informed by the old school that records will be passed onto the new school, including details of IEPs where appropriate.

Transfer to secondary school

The learning environment in secondary schools is different from primary settings in many ways. For example, in the primary school the child has a much clearer idea of what is expected by his or her teacher. In a primary school most lessons are taught by the class teacher; in the secondary school the pupil is taught by many different teachers who will not be as familiar with the child's special educational needs.

There is more movement around the school which may put the pupil with some SEN at a disadvantage, possibly through mobility difficulties, or due to confusion in getting to lessons on time, and because they will have to carry and organise their equipment. Therefore, the planning for pupils transferring to secondary schools must be very carefully executed. For example, making a book/folder with photographs of the school and key members of staff, to be looked at over the summer holiday, helps the child to remember where they might go and who they will work with. Visits should be made to acclimatise the pupil to the new building and meet some of the teachers, especially the SENCo. Make sure all records, including SEN records, are up-to-date and are transferred early enough in the summer term for those who need to know about the pupil's individual needs.

The school organising the departure needs to make every effort to contact the new school. A planning meeting at an annual review for a pupil with a statement, should include parents and, if possible, someone from the new school. Support services have a vital role in transition by helping the new school make plans. The receiving school must read all records in good time so that plans are in place before entry, especially for the more vulnerable pupils. This is usually well done for those with sensory or physical disabilities as support services and health personnel typically plan what equipment is needed and discuss mobility issues. Planning for pupils with more general difficulties is often much weaker. Yet for these pupils poor preparation may result in a setback to learning or, in extreme cases, such a traumatic start to the new school that the pupil never settles. In some schools members of the learning support department visit all tutor groups in the first two weeks of the new school year, in order to meet pupils with SEN and draw up a 'pen picture' of those learning characteristics which all staff need to know. Care should also be taken to note individual preferences and abilities but not lower expectations merely because the student appears on the SEN register.

Transition plans at 13+

The Code of Practice (2001), describes transition plan meetings which are usually held as part of the regular annual review meetings organised by the school. The responsibilities for running Annual Reviews and writing Transition Plans for those in Year 9 and above are made very clear.

> The Transition Plan should draw together information from a range of individuals within and beyond school in order to plan coherently for the young person's transition to adult life. Transition Plans when first drawn-up in Year 9 are not simply about post-school arrangements, they should also plan for on-going school provision, under the statement of SEN as overseen by the LEA.
>
> (Code of Practice, DfES 2001b: 9.51)

The head teacher must invite the agencies that may play a major role in the young persons life during post-school years, such as the 'Connexions Service'. This is a multi-agency service which provides advice and guidance to young people, along with access to personal development opportunities. Parents' and young peoples' views must be sought on transition planning. The Code of Practice (DfES 2001b) describes what should be addressed by transition plans (9.51–9.69).

The challenge of the Transition Plan lies in development of continuity of assessment, review and programme planning from school through further educational, vocational and personal preparation for a valued and productive adult life. The Code of Practice makes it very clear that the young person must be actively involved in the development of the Transition Plan and their views taken into account. As Gascoigne points out, this may be the first time that the young person is consulted without parents being present. She suggests that parents may find this period very stressful as their feelings are ambivalent. 'On the one hand they want their child to become as independent as possible, and on the other, they wish to extend their protection of them' (Gascoigne 1995: 38). Gascoigne and Russell emphasise how sensitive parents can be and how much support they will need from those working with them.

Transition plans start in Year 9 and continue annually until the young person leaves school. It is important that all professionals involved build good relationships with the young person and their families and give them all information about what is available in their local area. The process is usually carried out very thoroughly in special schools, but should be available to pupils with SEN in mainstream schools.

> LEAs must seek information from social services departments under Section 5 of the Disabled Persons (Services, Consultation and Representation) Act 1986, as to whether a young person with a statement under Part IV of the Education Act 1996 is disabled, (and so may require services from the local authority when leaving school).
>
> (Code of Practice, DfES 2001b: 9.58)

Children who have been looked after by the local authority until their 16th birthday will have a care plan and there will be a Connexions Personal Advisor (PA) for these young people. The care plan fulfils the same function as the Transition Plan. The Connexions service is responsible for overseeing the delivery of the Transition Plan, and the Connexions PA should coordinate its delivery. Details are provided in the SEN Toolkit, Section 10 (see also paragraphs 9.63 and 9.64 of the Code of Practice, DfES 2001b).

Post-16 transition to Further Education college

In order to help young people and their parents/carers, as well as school SENCos, support staff and other key personnel, it may help to compile a handbook which will include simple, straightforward information about applying for college courses offered, and other practical considerations such as claiming Disability Living

Allowance. Transport to college can also be an issue if the student cannot use public transport. The LA may be able to help with a taxi service.

Colleges should be approached with a view to including entry criteria for all courses in their prospectuses, including GNVQ Foundation and NVQ1, not just those where the needs of the accrediting body demand it. Admission to courses would then be based on fair and transparent procedures, and not on assumptions or subjective impressions. Colleges would benefit when planning provision, from year-on-year projections of those with specific types of disabilities. A high level of support in FE may be needed for students with statements. However, as the trend now is towards reducing the number of statements, it is even more important that secondary schools communicate information early, regarding all vulnerable students who might need support. Such support must be in place at the beginning of the course as the first few weeks are crucial in terms of student retention. Supported wheelchair access and supported physical care facilities may be required. Many other access issues must also now be considered, especially under the DRC Code of Practice Post-16 (DRC 2002a), which states that colleges have a duty not to discriminate against those with any kind of disability in their admissions procedures.

There is a need to make improvement in the level of training for both FE lecturers and learning support staff on issues relating to SEN and disability. The Further Education Funding Council (FEFC) now provides staff development materials in response to the findings of Inclusive Learning FEFC (Tomlinson report 1996). The further education world is very competitive, and as colleges become able to recruit higher ability students, market demand may lead to a phasing out of some current courses for SEN students. Restricted funding of colleges means that students with more severe disabilities will need additional support from the FEFC. Moreover, the remit of the health service to work with students needing adult level health care is confined to schools.

As a result of the Learning & Skills Act (2000) a national learning and skills council was set up for England. This council has a duty to have regard to the needs of people with difficulties and disabilities and to provide equal opportunities between disabled and non-disabled people. This Act, in conjunction with the SENDA and its Post-16 Code of Practice (DRC 2002a) and the SEN Code of Practice (DfES 2001b), gives a strong policy base for good practice to be developed in FE colleges.

Transition planning using the Connexions Services will be key to effective planning of further education provision. However, it is vital that the information gathered reaches all who are involved in the enrolment of students. The Connexions Service may be used as a bridge from schools or college to work placements. It must be remembered that the young persons' views are all important. Sometimes they do not want attention to be drawn to their differences by having individual support. Their permission must be sought before information is shared with staff. Personal plans with goal setting are now required for all Key Stage 4 students at potential risk of social exclusion. It may be helpful to invite a college tutor to the final school review to discuss the support available in the college. This can help reassure both student and parent to ease transition.

Under-16 students

Colleges are reporting that there is an increase in under 16-year-old students being transferred from schools, often for those with difficult to manage behaviour. Very careful planning will be required for these vulnerable younger students. As Sproson (2003) explains, successful placement in a college environment depends on the student's participation in the referral process, good preparation and the suitable appointment of a support liaison advisor. He further advises that FE placement will not be a suitable option for all such students.

CHAPTER 9

Managing Paperwork and Procedures
The Coordinating Role

This chapter links with Chapter 3 on identification and planning and looks at the coordinating role of the SENCo in relation to the paperwork and procedures required by the Code of Practice (2001) and SENDA (DfES 2001a). The SENCo has some responsibility for tracking the progress of pupils with SEN, and takes a lead role in organising annual reviews for those with statements. The Code of Practice has made great demands on SENCos in terms of resources of time and their management abilities. This chapter describes ideas gathered from practice about ways of organising paperwork, tracking pupil progress and working in partnership with pupils, parents and colleagues. The chapter also describes special situations in which SENCos might be asked to help prepare evidence for (1) SEN tribunals and (2) Ofsted inspections.

All of the above should be reflected in how roles and responsibilities are allocated and evaluated as part of the school's SEN policy as described in Chapter 2. One of the issues for large schools, particularly in the secondary phase, is how much of this responsibility can reasonably or efficiently be given to the SENCo and how the SENCo will collaborate and communicate with others – particularly those in the pastoral team, the head and governors.

The work described here is perceived as an important part of the coordinating role, though not necessarily to be carried out by the SENCo alone. The head has the ultimate responsibility to see that these tasks are carried out effectively and, in turn, must report to the governors on their effectiveness. The tasks required include:

- contributing to the review of the whole-school policy for SEN, or a section on SEN in the School Improvement Plan and contributing to the Self Evaluation Form (SEF) ensuring that SEN issues are included where appropriate;
- ensuring data is available for those on the graduated stages of the Code of Practice and those with statements;
- organising paperwork for a request for multi-disciplinary assessments;
- contributing to the Educational Advice for the statutory assessment when requested by the LA;
- setting of targets within two months of receipt of the statement – designing an IEP for each pupil with a statement in conjunction with relevant staff;
- holding annual reviews for pupils with statements; this is the responsibility of the head teacher, but in practice is often delegated to the SENCo;
- supporting the head if she/he is requested to attend a tribunal;
- supporting the head in preparation for an Ofsted inspection.

All of the above will require organisation skills and clarity of purpose and call on interpersonal skills when involved in dealing with a range of people; the child, parent, teacher and other professionals. This consultative work will be covered in more depth in the next chapter. This chapter will concentrate on the organisational and bureaucratic aspects of the work.

The management of the SEN records

The SEN record should contain, as a minimum, a list of pupils at each of the graduated stages. Many schools keep other information on this register, such as short notes about the type of LDDs each pupil may have, if English is their second language, and the date of the last IEP review. Monitoring the SEN register and checking how representative it is across classes, gender and ethnic groups may expose any undue bias.

Organisation of files

It may sound mundane or even trivial, but much rests on how and where files and records are stored, and how accessible these are to the SENCo and staff alike. There is no single correct way to do this; each school needs to design the system which works for them and then to make it clear within their policy document. Much record keeping is now electronic, but tracking data is an important part of the SENCo's role, along with others in the school. It is most important that, whether evidence is kept on paper or electronically, SENCos should carefully consider how best to track and keep evidence of individual progress. It is also important to ensure that SENCos and staff have easy access to information. In some schools access to electronic records may be limited due to lack of access to the main computer.

Organisation of IEP reviews

Of all the aspects of the Code of Practice, this can be the most challenging to schools. Running reviews is very time consuming for the class or subject teacher as well as for the SENCo. If parent and pupil views are to be fully incorporated, this too makes enormous demands on a school's resource of time, therefore, careful thought should be given when deciding who needs an IEP. The Code of Practice (2001) suggests that only those with significant additional needs should have IEPs, usually those on *School Action Plus* and above. Group IEPs may also be a solution for those with the more commonly occurring difficulties (see Chapter 3).

The whole strength of the graduated response depends on tracking progress in a regular, thorough manner. As this is now required for all pupils, it is up to schools to develop ways that work for teachers and pupils, while still complying with the main principles of the Code of Practice. These are to identify and meet the needs of all pupils and to give every child full access to the curriculum and life of the school. Good assessment leads to good teaching, so if used, the IEP process must work to improve teaching and learning outcomes.

The IEP as a process of continuous assessment

If an IEP is used, it must be envisaged as a process as well as a set of documents. Writing one beautiful plan will not suffice; it is the setting and evaluating of the targets *over time* that makes an IEP valuable to the pupil. The key questions are:

- What does *this* pupil need as a priority to help them make progress in the curriculum? What are the pupil's and the parents' views?
- What level has the pupil already reached? (state existing levels of attainment, particularly in literacy and numeracy, in as precise a way as possible). What can the child do? What are their strengths?

- What strategies/interventions have already been and/or are being used? What changes need to be made? This might include frequency and timing of support.
- What are the logical next steps to be achieved within the priority areas chosen (i.e. set targets)? These need to be decided with the pupil wherever possible.
- How will the information from the IEP inform lesson planning by the teacher?
- How will the targets be evaluated? If the targets are not set in precise enough terms, it will be impossible to know if they were or were not achieved.
- Decide who will monitor all of the above and how progress will be recorded.

School Action Plus review

A *School Action Plus* review can be used to return a pupil to *School Action*, if sufficient progress has been made, or it may be used to request a multi-professional assessment from the LA. Schools need to develop a policy on entry/exit criteria for use at *School Action Plus* reviews. Where a multi-disciplinary assessment is being considered, parents'/carers' views must be sought and the purpose explained in detail. The possibility that the LA (1) may not agree to the making of the assessment, or (2) may not issue a statement after examining the outcome, must be explained along with the parents' right to appeal.

School Action Plus is characterised by the use of multi-agency involvement. However, some schools may have teachers with specialist expertise, so may not require such advice. Those who have been involved with the child should contribute to this review. They will be asked for evidence as part of the assessment and their views are needed in this review. Parents can make a request for a multi-professional assessment independently of the school or support services, but the school continues to be required to give evidence.

Most LAs have set quite stringent criteria for requests for statutory assessments which they will have published, along with proformas they wish schools to complete. The Code of Practice states very clearly that it is the head teacher's responsibility to make the decision to request a formal assessment, unless a parent has already done so. However, this is usually done in close cooperation with the SENCo. The LA will need evidence of the pupil's needs and about what the school has already done to meet these. Schools will be asked to write the Educational Advice as their contribution to the formal assessment process. All the advice will be attached to the draft statement and will be part of the document known as the Statement (see Appendix 9) and Code of Practice (2001: 7).

Annual reviews

The full details of annual review procedures are published in Chapter 9 of the Code of Practice (2001). Every child who has a statement of SEN must have this statement reviewed by the LA at least annually. Reviews for those leaving school are an important part of transition planning (see Chapter 8) The Code of Practice states:

> The purpose of the annual review is to integrate a variety of perspectives in the child's progress and amend the statement to reflect newly identified needs and provision. The Annual Review should focus on what the child has achieved as well as on any difficulties that need to be resolved.
>
> (Code of Practice, 2001: 9.4)

Preparation of paperwork

Advanced planning is essential, as it takes time to collect reports for an annual review. At least two months in advance of the meeting the head must request written advice from:

- the child's parents/carers
- those the LA has specified
- those the head teacher considers appropriate.

These are likely to be the class and support teacher or assistant, any specialist teacher giving advice or an educational psychologist, and/or any health and social service professionals involved with the child.

Parents may need support on submitting their advice and may welcome a pre-review meeting, especially if it is the first annual review after the statement was made or at transition times when their child is due to change school. An informal meeting may prepare the parent for the much bigger and more formal review meeting. Parents usually find annual reviews stressful, so the preparation meeting can provide an opportunity to answer their questions and ensure they feel confident that their views have been noted.

The review meeting

Person Centred Planning is a way of empowering people to plan their future and organise services they need. Some LAs and schools are beginning to incorporate these ideas into the annual review process. The aim is to support the pupil and parents through preparation in the way the review is conducted. For example, these points should be covered:

- how the room is set out to put the child and parent/carer at ease;
- respecting the child and parents'/carers' preferred means of communication;
- inviting those present to record their view of the child's strengths and progress on charts round the room; start with positives about what we like and admire;
- consider a range of issues such as what's working/not working; what's important to the child and important to their health and support needs;
- acknowledging that people have different perspectives, but drawing these together into a time limited action plan showing what each person involved should aim to achieve;
- recording questions that remain unanswered.

(Personal communication from Colin Hardy 2007: SENSSA conference notes; see also Source List 1b)

After the review

The head must prepare the review report which summarises the outcomes of the review meeting and sets targets for the coming year. They then circulate this report to all those concerned with the review. The report must be sent to the LA by the end of term. The LA must then review the statement in the light of the report and may:

Recommend amendments to a statement if:
1 Significant new needs have emerged which are not recorded on the statement.
2 Significant needs which are recorded on the statement are no longer present.
3 The provision should be amended to meet the child's changing needs and the targets specified at the review meeting, or
4 The child should change schools, either at the point of transfer between school phases, for example infant to junior or primary to secondary, or
5 When a child's needs would more appropriately be met in a different school, for example by inclusion in the mainstream.

(Code of Practice, 2001: 9)

The SENDIST tribunal

The SEN tribunal was originally set up by the Education Act (1993). Since 2001 the tribunal has been called the Special Educational Needs and Disability Tribunal (SENDIST). The new title reflects responsibility for appeals brought under either special educational needs legislation or the Disability Discrimination Act (1995), as amended by the Special Educational Needs and Disability Act (2001). The tribunal has specific powers. Each tribunal is chaired by a lawyer, drawn from a list appointed by the Lord Chancellor. The tribunal is completed by two lay members, drawn from a list appointed by the Secretary of State. These members will have knowledge and experience of children with special educational needs or, in a disability appeal, expertise in aspects of disability. It considers parents' appeals against decisions of the LA about a child's special educational needs where the parents cannot reach agreement with the LA. The Code of Practice (2001) states that parents have the right to appeal to the SEN tribunal if they disagree with:

- the LA's decision not to assess and they, the parents, have been involved in requesting that assessment (Code of Practice, 7.90)
- the description of the child's needs in Part 2 of the Statement (description of special educational provision), and in Part 3 of the Statement (the school named, or if no school is named, that fact) or Part 4 of the Statement (Code of Practice, 8.108–8.110)
- the named change of school (e.g. at phase changes) (Code of Practice, 8.132)
- the LA's decision not to maintain a statement (Code of Practice, 8.120).

Parents may also use the tribunal if:

- after making a statutory assessment, the LA does not issue a statement but issues a 'note in lieu' (Code of Practice, 8.15)
- the LA refuses to reassess the child's SEN and the parents' request was made more than six months after any previous assessment (Code of Practice, 7.97).

Parents *cannot* use the SENDIST to complain about the way the LA is carrying out an assessment, providing help as stated, or the way the school is meeting their child's SEN. Nor can they use the tribunal to appeal against the description of non-educational provision in Parts 5 and 6 of the statement.

In all cases where parents disagree with the LA decision there must be ample opportunity for discussion with an officer and any relevant professional. The LA must inform the parents of their right to appeal to the SENDIST. The parents should also be given information about parent partnership and disagreement services and informed that their right to appeal cannot be affected by any disagreement resolution procedure (Code of Practice, 8). Parents are increasingly using tribunals to ask for placements in special schools, due to the feeling that mainstream schools have failed their child. Although the intention was not to make them confrontational or to populate them with lawyers, this has often been the case. Parents do not need to be represented by a lawyer, but many have chosen to do so, although legal aid is only available for preparation and not presentation of the case.

The school's role in tribunal cases

School staff, such as the head teacher, SENCo or year head, may be asked to attend as witnesses by either the LA or the parents. Where a member of staff is reluctant to attend as a witness voluntarily, the individual may be required to attend through an order issued by the tribunal. School staff may be expected to provide detailed information about the child's special educational needs (or disability), the actions taken by the school to meet these identified needs and evidence of the progress made by the pupil. They may also have to respond to questions from the tribunal members, parents or the LA on issues such as how the school allocates their resources from the SEN budget, how support is organised and how the curriculum is differentiated to match the IEP targets.

It is wise therefore to have an agreed policy, not only for ordinary complaints to the school, but for cases where the parent may appeal against an LA decision – whether this is a decision not to assess or re-assess a child, not to issue a statement, or about the actual contents of a statement. In preparing its response to the appeal, the LA may expect the SENCo to help produce detailed evidence in the form of well-kept records, showing both the pupil's progress and the types of intervention and support given by the school. The pupils' and parents' views over time will be an important part of this evidence. Class teachers may sometimes be required to produce evidence of curriculum work of the pupil.

Sometimes schools may agree with the parents' appeal to the tribunal against the LA. In other situations schools might agree with the LA. In both cases the school can feel caught between the LA and the parent, and so the whole context of the tribunal hearing and its preparation can cause stress for all concerned. Where parents have appealed against an LA decision, there are two very important requirements for the school. Firstly, although IEPs may not now be used, it is still essential to be able to give evidence of how assessments, interventions and progress tracking have been carried out. Secondly, everything should have been done to maintain normal professional relationships with the parents, or their 'named person'. Staff need not agree with everything about the parents' appeal or the LA's response, indeed the school should at all times focus its contribution, supported by evidence upon factual information about the educational needs of the child and the provision necessary to ensure success in learning. School staff should be aware throughout the process of appeal that they have to continue to work closely with the parents after the hearing and that the LA and parents must comply with the Tribunal Order.

The tribunal process is very stressful and lengthy for parents, and it is not always clear whether it benefits the child to any great extent. Parent partnership schemes have been very effective in offering mediation and consultation to parents who disagree with school or LA decisions. The government now expects LAs to take positive action to try to resolve issues without recourse to the tribunal. However, this must not deny the parents' rights to appeal if they so wish.

Preparation by the SENCo for an Ofsted inspection

The whole emphasis from Ofsted has now shifted to school self-evaluation. The responsibility is the school's to produce a Self Assessment Form (SEF) based on its strengths and weaknesses. From reading the SEF, the lead inspector chooses which issues should be further pursued. This means that if no aspect of SEN is identified as an issue by the school, then the SENCo may not see the team. The main job of the SENCo is to ensure that his/her contribution to the SEF is accurate and that the impact of the intervention/support used by the school can be clearly demonstrated. SENCos need to be able to analyse data, especially from www.raiseonline.org (Ofsted/DCSF) so that they can see how well SEN pupils are doing, both within the school and across similar schools locally and nationally.

The following information might be useful if a SENCo meets with the inspection team:

- the school must be able to show evidence for all children as to how progress is tracked and monitored;
- the SEN records showing information about the number of pupils on *School Action* and *School Action Plus* as well as those with statements;

- the SEN policy, giving information about the school as listed in Schedule 1 (see Appendix 2a). This is to include evidence of how this is monitored and evaluated annually;
- staffing information: qualifications and job descriptions for SENCo and support staff;
- links with other schools or colleges, including how records and information are passed on to the receiving school;
- information about the use of outside agencies and services and how liaison is managed;
- targets and action points from previous inspections and the school's SEN annual policy statements to parents;
- information about the SEN budget. SENCos should know their own department's budget and be able to discuss the school's priorities for resourcing SEN.

Knowing about the SEN budget

As discussed in Chapter 2, the head and governors continue to hold overall responsibility for determining the policy and approach to SEN and for setting up appropriate funding and staffing arrangements. The governors' annual report must inform parents about the success of the SEN policy and any significant changes and the allocation of resources over the previous year to pupils with SEN. It is not the SENCo's role to determine budgets or policies, but it will be useful if their advice is sought by governors and if, in turn, the SENCo understands the main principles which the governors apply in deciding how resources will be allocated *between and amongst* pupils with SEN.

Many SENCos report that gaining access to budget and resource information is difficult. The funds which are devolved from the LA to the school under the LMS schemes are known and in the public domain. Some of these are worked out by the number and age of pupils on role (Age/Pupil Weighted: APW), others by the funding allocated for additional needs. These may be related to the proxy indicator of those eligible to free school meals or on other indices decided by the LA such as those on the SEN register or frequent pupil movement between schools. But how these funds are used is decided by the governing body.

Monitoring and reviewing the school's SEN policy

As discussed in more detail in Chapter 2, there is an expectation within the requirements for SEN policies as listed in the Code of Practice and expanded on in Circular 6/94, that every school will review their SEN policy annually. In practice, schools have often left this task until an Ofsted inspection is due.

Unfortunately, it also seems that many schools have not set targets or success criteria, so a new SENCo may have to do this for the first time when wishing to set up a review cycle. It is important to recognise that a review may cover all aspects of policy in a general manner and then focus on one or two areas in greater depth.

These priority areas may arise from external inspections or from staff in schools identifying some aspect that needs improvement or has not previously been covered (see Activity 6).

Summary

This chapter has described the core of the SENCo's administrative work which is:

- the maintenance of paperwork and organisation of review procedures associated with the Code of Practice including preparation for tribunal cases;
- the monitoring of individual and group planning and associated curriculum planning and assessment for all pupils with SEN;

- data monitoring and preparation of paperwork or information to feed into reviews of the school policy or development plan, or for an Ofsted inspection.

The prime aim of all of these tasks is to improve the opportunities for pupils with SEN to learn effectively, access the curriculum, make progress and be valued as full members of the school community. The SENCo can help make this happen if they can both organise efficiently and work in a supportive way with all concerned. This consultative role will be considered in the next chapter.

CHAPTER 10

Working with People
The Consultative Role

This chapter looks at these aspects of the SENCo's consultative role:

- *working with pupils*: considering pupil perspectives and rights
- *working in partnership with parents/carers*: dealing with stress and complaints
- *working with colleagues*: giving support and training
- *working with governors*.

Each section will look both at the personal skills of the SENCo and features of the whole school approach, which together contribute to effective development of the consultative role. Everyone looks to the SENCo for support, advice and even counselling. How much of this rather less formal work any particular SENCo can do, depends on a number of factors. The first of these factors is the SENCo's own feeling of confidence. This will be stronger when based on a feeling of competence built up through knowledge and skills gained from experience and training. It takes time to build up this confidence and competence so as to be in a position to support others and act as a change agent in a school. The second of the factors which will enhance and facilitate the consultative role are the school's policies and its ethos. The following aspects should be considered when reviewing policies:

- Is there an honest, open attitude towards partnership with parents/carers?
- To what extent do all those within the school community feel able to express their opinions and ideas, and participate in decision-making as appropriate?
- Are pupils' perspectives valued in the way policies and procedures for the whole population in the school have been developed?
- Is the responsibility for the learning and well-being of pupils with LDDs seen as the shared responsibility of everyone on the staff?
- Are staff valued and given praise by senior management?
- Do governors understand policy and practice, and contribute effectively to strategic planning and decision-making?

Enhancing pupil perspectives

To achieve an understanding of the pupil's own view of their school experience and their educational needs requires an ability on behalf of the teacher to change perspective. Teachers have to let go of their position of authority, for a short time, and view the world of the classroom from the pupil's point of view. This may best be done through becoming a careful observer for certain times and taking detailed notes. If someone else can manage the class for a short session while this observation takes place, it may be easier to be free to observe.

Learning to be a skilled observer

Learning observation skills gives teachers a useful tool for assessment and general problem-solving. Observation can be for set times (e.g. ten minutes) or of specific events or of a specific context, such as the playground. Starting the observation without a precise focus may be possible, but increasingly focusing on an intended feature may give more insight. If pupil perspectives are the focus, this may need to be combined with interview techniques. There are a number of observation techniques given in Appendix 10a. Accurate observation for as little as ten minutes, if focused and prepared, can give insights into a particular area of concern, whether an individual pupil or a group. Always remember that observation will be affected by bias, so if more than one adult can observe to a prepared schedule the results may be more reliable.

Using other techniques

Another way to get a pupil's perspective is, of course, to ask the pupil to talk about or express their views. This can be by direct questions about an aspect of their work such as reading or homework, or it can be by more open-ended questioning about school or friends. Open-ended interviewing is difficult for some teachers to do, partly because of time constraints, partly because it is a skill to be learnt. Sometimes other adults, ancillary helpers or support professionals may fare better because they may offer less threat to pupils or have time to see pupils in a more relaxed environment. The whole class can be given exercises to evaluate an aspect of their own learning, possibly to give ratings about how confident they feel about various aspects of their learning. For younger pupils, faces with different expressions can be used to rate answers instead of words (see Appendix 10b).

It is more difficult to gain a view of pupil perspective where the pupil lacks the language to express their thoughts and feelings in words. In these cases observations from more than one adult may need to be combined to give a feel for the pupil's perspective. This can be achieved by looking at pupil reactions to activities, teaching approaches and at resources and events. Ancillary helpers' and parents' observations about different aspects of the pupil's development and feelings of self-worth are very helpful in putting together a joint perspective. The use of video cameras and tape recorders can help collect valuable data in cases where more direct questioning is difficult – for example, the developmentally young, or pupils with language impairment. These would not be kept as a long-term record, but might help analyse complex observations. The issue of parental permission for video use has become increasingly important. Some schools ensure that such permission is obtained for pedagogical purposes, when the pupil is admitted to the school. Drawings and symbolic representations of situations as perceived during play can all add to the teacher's understanding of pupil perspectives.

The above approaches take time, for just one child, and cannot be used for all the pupils in a class or on the SEN register. Different methods can be selected for different children and at different times. It is useful however if, as part of training sessions, teachers can practise some of the skills required in collecting and collating information. This will enhance their ability to look at pupil perspectives. For some teachers, the exercise of *really* trying to understand one pupil, from a child's point of view, is a revelation.

School policy: taking pupil perspectives into account

The Code of Practice (DfES 2001b: 3) discusses pupil participation in some detail. Other guidance can be found in the SEN Toolkit (Section 4). Children and young people have the right to be involved in making decisions and exercising choices. They have a unique knowledge of their needs and their views should be listened to and taken into account. The law has strengthened pupil rights to be involved in decision-making and planning meetings such as reviews of statements. However, teachers may still find it difficult to be sure that they have heard the 'true pupil voice'. Regular conferencing times when the pupils' views are taken down can be built into review procedures for IEPs or given to all pupils. The Records of Achievement approach to recording progress, as part of the school's assessment policy, will enhance the work of those operating in special needs. As part of the review of the SEN policy, the following questions need to be asked:

- Do we take account of pupil viewpoints and perspectives?
- Do we have procedures and times when we can note pupil viewpoints and perspectives?
- Do pupil views and perspectives influence policy-making in the school?
- Do we seek the views of pupils with a range of LDD?

In some schools, it is expected that all units of teaching and learning will include some opportunities for pupil feedback, not only on what they have learnt, but also on what teaching approaches were most successful. This is an approach advocated in *Leading on Inclusion* materials (DfES 2005).

The Disability Equality Duty requires schools to consult with parents of pupils with LDD and parents who themselves have LDD. They must also consult with pupils, staff, governors and other stakeholders about the impact all school policies and practices have on those with LDDs, and how improvements could be made. The process and outcomes of such consultation must be produced as a Disability Equality Scheme and Action Plan.

SENCos need to be aware, when considering the pupil voice, of the disproportionate number of pupils with SEN who are excluded permanently or for a fixed term. As SENDIST is likely to overturn exclusion if a pupil's special needs have not been met, SENCos need to work closely with pupils at risk of exclusion and their families to take preventative steps, and in the event, to give an account of all the support that was given and why it failed.

Working in partnership with parents/carers

Parents are defined under the Children Act (1989) as those who have parental responsibility for the child or who have care of the child (full description in Appendix 10c). The school's policy should contain a clear statement of the arrangements for ensuring close working partnerships with parents of children with special educational needs. This will mean incorporating parents' views in assessment and reviews and ensuring parents are fully informed about the school's procedures and are made welcome in the school. Much of this will be achieved if a policy for parents of all pupils is inclusive and enhances participation. SEN policy should not be an add-on, but an integral part of the school's general way of working with parents.

Just as understanding the pupils' viewpoints needed a change of perspective for the teacher, so often does understanding the parents' or carers' viewpoint. If a true partnership with parents is to be established, then the teacher or the SENCo needs to learn to listen to and value the parents' expertise about their own child or their concerns about his or her progress. (In linguistically diverse schools and communities, parents may need an interpreter.) To do this effectively, it is necessary to learn new skills. Teachers are good at expressing themselves and activating ideas. They may not be quite as good as listeners. Listening effectively in the consultative role is a skill to be learnt and practised.

Empathic listening

In this mode the listener obeys certain ground rules. These are:

- keep eye contact;

- keep still, do not distract your listener by fiddling with pens, etc.;
- keep your own comments to a minimum, such as 'I see', 'right', 'I understand' and 'yes';
- if longer comments are required, make these reflective, i.e. feedback the main point as you understood it, so it can be checked: use these comments to summarise points and check that you have understood what was said;
- don't be afraid to feed back feelings as well as facts: 'That must have made you angry', 'You were upset by . . .'.

Such listening sessions will need time limits, which should be set in advance if possible: 'We've got half an hour, please tell me your concerns and worries, we will try to find some answers.' Check that the parent is happy for you to take notes. Often it is not a good idea to do this if you are really trying to listen, as you cannot keep eye contact and write notes. It may be a good idea to make time to summarise at the end of the session and agree a few points which can be written down. Establishing a feeling of trust is more important than note-taking at this point. Once the problem has been identified and the parent feels they were listened to, it is possible to move into a *problem-solving mode*.

Problem-solving

As a first step, this requires that the problem has been clearly identified. Next, actions can be jointly planned with the parent to try to solve the problem. Problem-solving again needs a sensitive approach from the teacher, while setting boundaries for what is achievable in school within limited resources. Wherever possible, the parents/carers will feel more of a partner if they can suggest ideas to be discussed, perhaps offer to help in some way at home or in school. Joint targets can then be set and a date to review progress made. Copies of written notes of meetings should be given to parents wherever possible.

Cultural awareness

Families and communities have different attitudes to having a child with LDD; some may be 'in denial', or feel ashamed. Cultural differences will need to be recognised and all those involved be sensitive to these. Experienced staff and the EMA (Ethnic Minority Achievement) team should be consulted if uncertain of how to interact in the child's best interests. If interpreters are used they should be helped to understand the language and concept of SEN.

Developing partnerships

If schools have listened to parents when developing other policies, then parents' perspectives will already be reflected. Parents of pupils with SEN are however particularly vulnerable. Some parents are not always confident enough to ask for their views to be taken into account, or even know their rights. It is therefore essential that the SENCo gives parents information about these rights. Parents need to have the graduated assessment procedure explained. They need to know about LA services which may be called upon to support their child. School provision for SEN also needs to be explained.

Parents may sometimes have feelings of anger, guilt and frustration over finding that their child is not making expected progress. To make a partnership with such parents requires the SENCo to have skills of assertiveness and the ability to set limits, in particular, knowing how to say 'no' and knowing how to limit time spent. If the relationship is not dealt with carefully, a confrontation rather than a partnership can occur. As Dale (1996) explains, parents can go through a 'psychic shock' when they first hear of their child's disability. The first phase may only last a day or so, at which time they need sympathy and understanding. Next, information is required to help them orientate. The next step will be to use a problem-solving approach to help parents come to terms with the new situation. Emphatic listening can still help establish a rapport followed by a structured problem-solving session. If the parents feel they really have been listened to and their viewpoints taken into account, they will feel calmer and able to look for joint practical solutions. If, however, their feelings seem irrational and solutions are beyond the resources of the school, it may be necessary to seek help either from other members of the school, the head for example, or outside professionals.

Almost all parents can be brought into a partnership situation. Difficulties arise when promises are broken, resources do not arrive, the pupil is absent intermittently or for long periods, or staff are inconsistent in following the school's SEN policy. In many of these cases the teacher's ability to work in partnership with parents dwindles. Parents' own adult needs cannot fully be addressed by the school, but it is possible to get a personal referral for help. The format of the CAF may also help SENCos with this assessment process in future.

Some SENCos have found that setting up parent support groups within the school has enabled parents to share expertise and develop skills, particularly for managing children with BESD. Such groups are sometimes facilitated by outside parenting skills trainers.

The questions SENCos need to keep in mind when working with parents are:

- What is a possible outcome of this meeting which will benefit the child?
- What resources are available from the school or the community to support this child and parent?
- What is achievable in the immediate future, and in the more distant future?

Being able to summarise the answers to these questions and feed back to the parents in a positive manner will be a way of recording the meeting.

Dealing with complaints

> Schedule 1, Regulation 2 (1): 1.12 states that the school SEN policy must include a section on how complaints will be dealt with. The policy should make clear to parents and children with SEN how they can make a complaint about the provision made for their child at the school and how that complaint will be dealt with by the school.

Schools usually have a general complaints system, but will need to give particular attention to SEN complaints. Often it is the class teacher or the SENCo to whom the parent first turns. This is the best action if the matter can be dealt with easily. It should be kept clearly in mind that the head teacher has the final responsibility for the school along with the governors. It is important therefore that procedures are clearly set out and published, and not left to chance. If schools make sure parents are fully informed throughout the assessment procedures and given access to the LA Parent Partnership Scheme as early as possible, it should be possible to allay fears and avoid complaints. The SEN Toolkit (Section 2) gives further information about Parent Partnership services. Ultimately, parents may have recourse to the SEN Disability Tribunal (SENDIST) if they are not satisfied with the school's actions.

Supporting colleagues

The needs of teachers have to be met if they in turn are to meet the needs of children, especially those children who are more difficult to teach. Galloway (1985) defined children with special needs as those children that caused teachers stress, either because they couldn't learn and make progress as expected, or because they could not conform to the norms of behaviour expected by the teacher. Teacher stress has been exacerbated by pressures of league tables and performance management. Successful teachers are often seen as those whose pupils achieve or exceed national expectations in attainment. Those with learning and behaviour difficulties can impact negatively on teacher self-image.

If the school is set up to support staff and provide them with ways of dealing with stressful situations collaboratively, the role of the SENCo will be a more effective part of this process. Where the school is not as supportive to teachers, pupils or parents as it should be, the consultative role for the SENCo will be much harder. He or she will have to choose those parts of the 'system' which can be worked with to achieve some success. The consultative role will have to begin with small actions wherever possible. This is in order to preserve the SENCo's own health and ability to cope with what is already a very complex job.

It is better to find one colleague who can be positively supported and helped to gain confidence and competence, than to try to do too much too fast. Don't expect too much change to occur too quickly. Where the system is more developed and there are already many positive features, such as many colleagues who have gained competence in meeting individual needs, working with parents and working collaboratively with others, then the scale of what can be achieved will be greater and the rate of change faster.

Much of what has been said in the previous sections applies to working successfully with colleagues. They too need someone to share concerns, so listening skills will apply here, as will problem-solving strategies. Often colleagues only need to be reassured that they are doing the right thing. Being able to describe their problem, express their concerns and anxieties will be sufficient to produce the feeling of being supported. It may be wise to follow this up by observation of the child or group in question. Fuller assessment may be part of the solution. An interview with pupil and parents may be indicated.

It is not the SENCo's role to know all answers to all questions. What they can do is to facilitate the *problem-solving abilities* of their colleagues and help them find solutions which they feel will work. These solutions may require the SENCo to work collaboratively with the class or child, or they may be to request precise advice on strategies on resources. Being able to enter into productive dialogues with colleagues is *the skill* the SENCo will need to develop most. It is, of course, more likely that the SENCo will also have knowledge of a particular strategy or resource to help a particular child, if they have experience of a wide range of SEN themselves or are knowledgeable about LA resources. With greater inclusion, SENCos are having to be aware of a wide range and depth of need. Through the Internet, all SENCos have access to a wide range of specialist advice and organisations. A staff SEN library can also provide a valuable resource.

The SENCo's role in supporting in-service training for SEN

The TTA Standards document (1998) stated that one of the SENCo's roles in leading and managing staff is to advise on, contribute to, or coordinate the professional development of staff to increase their response to pupils with SEN and to provide support and training of newly qualified teachers. Robertson (1999) also suggests the SENCo may be the member of staff best suited to induct newly qualified teachers. Initial teacher training will in future include aspects of working with LDD.

Supporting classroom teachers

Hanko (1995) explores in depth how staff development groups working with an outside consultant or a specially trained member of staff can work together in a problem-solving mode. Building on her work in both primary and secondary schools, developed over a number of years, she explains the purpose of such staff groups. Each session focuses on a specific child and, through sharing the knowledge of the teachers present and the skills they already possess, the group helps the teachers to find answers which will improve the situation and help the child cope better. Hanko says that by helping teachers realise the depth of knowledge they already possess about the learning process, the curriculum and child development, their objectivity is restored and confidence gained. She suggests that knowledge can be shared about the child, the whole classroom group in relation to the child, the teacher–pupil interaction and the therapeutic potential in the day-to-day curriculum.

The skills can be shared about:

- gauging the needs of a specific case from the behaviour displayed;
- making special bridging efforts to reach the child's 'teachable self';
- providing a consistent setting of new learning experiences likely to meet the needs gauged;
- if possible involving the child's parents and, if necessary, colleagues (fellow teachers and members of other professions) as genuine partners.

(Hanko 1995: 62)

She further suggests that by working on the underlying issues, the whole group of teachers develop problem-solving skills which they can use in other cases. Cleese, Daniels and Norwich (1997) also offer a model of teacher support involving self-referral and a solution-focused approach shared with colleagues.

It is often seen as central to the SENCo's role to take the lead in in-service sessions on the various aspects of SEN. Just how feasible this is again depends on the existing knowledge and competence level of the SENCo themselves. Many aspects of SEN policy and procedures can be dealt with in-house by the SENCo. It needs to be recognised, however, that the more specialist areas may not be known by anyone in one school and it is then that help needs to be brought in from outside services or professionals. SENCos may also wish to set up information corners in the staff room and provide all staff with a folder. This could include guidance on how the graduated response will be operated in the school and how contacts to outside agencies can be made.

Working with governors

As governors have a number of legal duties regarding SEN, most schools have a governor or a committee with responsibility for provision for children and young people with LDD. Governors need a high degree of awareness of SEN and disability legislation and an understanding of how this applies in practice, although much of the day-to-day implementation of their SEN duties is delegated to the head teacher and then on to the SENCo. As the SENCo is an invaluable source of information, establishing a relationship between SENCo and the governors is important. Regular meetings, at least termly, should be scheduled to brief governors on salient issues; to update them on changing patterns of need within the school and the best provision to make. The SENCo might sometimes attend a governors' committee meeting, or the SEN governor(s) might spend time in school familiarising themselves with the range of special educational needs, provision made, its impact and cost-effectiveness.

Ideally, the SENCo and governing body will work together within a whole school strategy towards the inclusion and success of children and young people with LDD in all aspects of school life. The SENCo, as a manager, may have an important role in advising governors of the best ways of consulting adults and children in the school community with LDD, in line with the Disability Equality Duty. The SENCo will also recognise that there is a raft of legislation relating to equalities for which governors are also responsible, including gender issues, race issues, protection of gay and lesbian staff and students, support for gifted and talented children with SEN, and the development of community cohesion, all of which will have a relationship to issues regarding LDD. The SENCo should see SEN issues in relation to these aspects of equality and help governors to understand the links and make coherent decisions.

As governors also agree the school budget and staffing decisions, the shrewd SENCo will be explicit about costs of resources, including teaching assistants, hardware and software, and modifications necessary to buildings and equipment, while ensuring that there is a convincing and evidence-based rationale for any new proposal. Governors must evaluate the impact of any provision that is made and it may be incumbent on the SENCo to supply appropriate data and qualitative information. For example:

- on the comparative attainment of pupils with different types of LDD;
- the participation of such children in school activities, including extra-curricular activities;
- information on any barriers to inclusion and achievement that pupils, staff or parents/carers have identified through consultation;
- the satisfaction of parents/carers with the provision made for their children.

Implementing the Disability Discrimination Act in Schools and Early Years Settings (DfES 2006b) gives guidance towards this evaluation process. Although SENCos may supply the information required by governors, who need to describe changes to the SEN policy and its effectiveness, and the progress of the Accessibility Plan or Disability Equality Scheme, it is governors who are responsible for writing and publishing the annual report.

Summary

This chapter has explored in some detail many of the consultative tasks that a SENCo is likely to carry out across a year. What any particular SENCo can manage of all these tasks will depend on time allocated to their role and to the support of others, the head teacher in particular.

CHAPTER 11

Working Together towards Inclusive Practice

Inclusion became the term in general use at the end of the twentieth century, replacing that of integration. Integration focused on the individual pupil, while inclusion is concerned with whole-school issues, challenging all forms of discrimination. Government documents promoted further inclusion within mainstream schools where parents wanted it and appropriate support could be provided, but admitted that the challenge this would produce for schools should not be underestimated and that solutions should be pragmatic and put the needs of individual children first. It continued by saying,

> Inclusion is a process not a fixed state. It should mean the participation of all pupils in learning which leads to the highest possible achievement and the participation of young people in the full range of social experiences and opportunities once they have left school.
> (DfEE 1998: 23)

Florian (1998) agreed that there was a gap between policy and implementation which should be acknowledged and addressed. She said that, if inclusion is the opportunity for people with a disability to participate fully in all activities that typify everyday society, this transcends the concept of normalisation. This is an important idea, because it means changing attitudes so that those with disabilities are not treated as a minority group, labelled and given special treatment. It means *including* activities for everyone which previously might have been seen as 'only for a disabled group'.

The drive for full inclusion had became a bit like a religious revival for some writers and speakers, especially those who used the social model or adopted the human rights position drawn from disability politics. Many writers then tried to unpack the term inclusion and to recognise its complexity. Robertson, for example, argued that while the social model had much to contribute to the theory and practice of inclusion, it provided a 'flawed explanatory framework for bringing change within education's complexity and contradiction' (Robertson 2001: 191). Robertson gives examples of problems to be solved which include:

- the failure to recognise that specialist teacher knowledge and skills are an essential part of more inclusive provision; (the TDA announced late in 2007 that they plan to develop SEN specialist training as a priority area in its next tri-annual cycle);
- the recognition that schools cannot work alone when continually being bombarded with conflicting demands from the government.

Inclusive schools

Ever since the Warnock Report and the 1981 Act were published, the emphasis has been on encouraging ordinary schools to increase their capacity to offer a full education of those with SEN. The government has adopted the term inclusion and embedded it within its Standards Agenda. A closer examination of this shows that this agenda is about school improvement and raising standards for all children and young people; the assumption being that by improving levels of achievement, those with LDD will benefit. However, as Allan (2003) argues 'education policies operate within a regime of accountability which is ineffective, inefficient and unjust'. A school achieving well on dimensions of inclusion may not be seen as successful when judged by the market-forces criteria of league tables and test scores. Schools alone cannot achieve the change needed for an inclusive system. As Fullan (2003) proposes, change must happen on the three levels of government, local district and school. Fullan explores what he calls complexity theory in depth (see Source List 1b).

One idea Fullan discusses is that of a learning community, where everyone is willing to learn together. Translating this into the inclusion debate means developing an ethos where everyone's contribution is valued and respected, using the views of pupils, parents, TAs and teachers in everyday problem solving and in longer-term policy making. This could also mean building partnerships between schools, especially between special and mainstream schools. Some of the most successful inclusion projects have occurred where local authorities set an agenda and develop policies which support schools and their teachers, offering extensive and ongoing training for SENCos and specialist training for teachers. These local authorities also help schools develop their own polices and practice with positive encouragement. This all requires strong commitment and leadership.

MacGilchrist and Buttress (2005) describe a 'Learning to Learn' project carried out as a partnership between five primary schools, their LA (Redbridge), and the Institute of Education. They built a networked learning community to transform learning and teaching in a rigorous, but creative way. A 'we can if' approach to inclusion was developed through strong leadership and the shared belief that all children have the capacity to learn. The Redbridge project focused on changing to a learning orientation to balance the previous performance orientation. However, the evaluation showed that concentration on learning also enhanced performance as judged by outside agencies.

Evidence from Ofsted's annual report 2005–6, using the five ECM outcomes, showed that schools whose achievement is good or outstanding, are also those where pupils are keen to learn.

The role of special schools

One commonly held view of inclusion indicated that schools must change so that *all* children can participate in the full life of their community by attending mainstream schools. This made the role of special schools problematical. By 2004 the government recognised the threat the inclusion agenda had become to special schools. Their important role was recognised, both as specialist establishments which could support certain vulnerable children and as partners with mainstream schools where expertise could be shared.

Warnock argues that 'what is needed is that all children should be included within the common educational project, not that they should be included under one roof' (Warnock 2005: 36). She also promotes the concept of small specialist schools, arguing that 'the pursuit of equality at school may be taking whatever steps that are necessary now to ensure greater opportunities later on' (Warnock 2005: 37). Tutt (2007b) thinks that the ECM agenda has refocused on individual needs and where these can best be met. The future should, she suggests, see all types of provision as part of the same service, with short-term or dual-roll placements becoming more common.

Inclusion in the learning process

O'Brien argues that 'the key component of an inclusive school is not the total sum of those included, (being there), but the duty to provide inclusive learning, (learning there)' (O'Brien 2001: 48). By examining what he calls 'hard cases', O'Brien shows that inclusion can be a risky operation for some pupils and teachers. He adds that it is only when verifiable evidence showing that classrooms too are inclusive, may we be on the way to achieving inclusion.

Wedell (2005) discussing the dilemma of inclusion, says that it is the rigidity of systems that hamper inclusion, citing as examples; statement procedures, school timetables and staffing, and the use of class teaching rather than more flexible groupings. He suggests that a higher level of flexibility in the way teaching and learning take place will be necessary if the aims of inclusive education are to be realised.

> Universal traditional class grouping of all children for all learning can no longer be seen as a relevant way to achieve the aims of inclusion. Pursuit of inclusion can no longer be synonymous with joint learning for all pupils in all situations.
>
> (Wedell 2005: 9)

Hornby (2001) stated that the priority for children with SEN must be that they access a curricula which is appropriate for them. For secondary pupils in particular, Hornby feels that there is a duty to teach skills which prepare the young person to be included in life after school, and in particular the world of work. Extended schools and services, an important part of the ECM agenda, is about building partnerships within a community, thus empowering them to identify needs and priorities. Holley (2007), of the TDA, believes that the nature of multi-agency approach to learning will offer faster help to pupils who need it.

Allan (2003) used the term productive pedagogies to point out ways in which inclusive practice could be improved. These include heightened intellectual demands on students, connecting to their lives outside school and recognising difference. Improved professional development which enables teachers to 'participate in a professional learning community within their schools' (Allan 2003: 175). She also points out that it is necessary to live with the tensions that inclusion brings and make positive connections between perspectives.

Child and young people's perspectives

> Inclusive education is about responding to diversity, it is about listening to unfamiliar voices, being open to empowering all members and celebrating differences in dignified ways.
>
> (Barton 1997: 233)

The perspective of those who are included, the child and young person themselves should be considered when discussing inclusion. Allan (1999) writes about the ways that pupils actively seek inclusion, working on themselves and their mainstream peers to make inclusion happen. She adds that pupils need to be helped to cope with the real solutions in which they find themselves and seek ways of overcoming the disability barriers which remain. Teachers might help, she thinks, by guiding pupils to explore their sense of self-expressed desires rather than their needs, possibly negotiating strategies which recognise both needs and desires, for example, by providing support which does not disturb peer interaction.

Research which elicits the young persons' views reveals the details of their hopes and fears. DRC funded research by Lewis *et al.* (2006) used case studies to explore the key concerns and priorities of disabled children, young people and their families. The aim was also to identify barriers faced by young disabled people in education following the implementation of SENDA (2001). The themes of this research were:

* independence and autonomy
* educational services and environments
* knowledge and assertion of rights
* attitudes, ambitions and aspirations.

The outcome of this research led to recommendations to policy makers and for practitioners. For this latter group important points included:

- responding as well as listening to the views of children and young people
- importance of discussing the use of additional staff on a regular basis
- general openness between schools and parents concerning use of extra help
- importance of giving information about pupils' needs to temporary staff.

SENCos and inclusion

SENCos and teachers already know that inclusion is not a simple one-dimensional concept. At a strategic planning level, being an inclusive school requires an attitude of mind from all who work in it which effects the overall ethos of the school, its systems and organisation and the well-being of all within. Inclusion depends on managing effective partnerships between teachers, support staff and parents; recognising each other's contributions. At another level, inclusion means that the curriculum on offer and the teaching that takes place in classrooms allows for diversity of learning styles, pace and focus. Such quality teaching allows pupils to participate fully in the learning process. At the third level, that of the individual child, inclusion is likely to be about friendship, self-esteem and relationships with the peer group.

One role the SENCo holds will be that of a 'change agent' within the school as an organisation. Working towards more inclusive practice is a process which will be ongoing. If it is to be effective, other teachers will need to be involved and senior management will need to give their support.

The purpose of this final chapter is to examine the SENCo's role in its totality within the context of whole-school development. Schools are being challenged to become more effective by setting targets for improvement against national and local benchmarks. The SENCo will have an important part to play in a school's development by keeping the quality of teaching and learning for *all* pupils on the agenda. How does the child with special educational needs fare in this search for school improvement? Are they to be welcomed as part of a diverse community and valued for their contribution and achievements; or does the focus on publishing results and ever improving standards make schools afraid to include these pupils on their roll?

One characteristic of a good school is that it has established good management of resources which maximise the potential effectiveness of the whole institution. Resources of time, people and equipment will be required to meet the identified range of pupils with special needs. Policies will require strategic planning by those in management to include the careful monitoring of these resources. This policy and resource allocation must be clearly understood by everyone, including parents/carers.

However, a successful inclusion policy is as much to do with attitudes and values as resources. Developing effective inclusive education remains a challenge to most schools, even when it is a part of their mission. 'Society is made up of other people's children', was a remark frequently made by Joan Sallis when talking to teachers. By this she meant that we cannot afford to educate only the high achievers or the easy-to-teach children, because every child will be part of our future.

The SENCo should always consider the individual needs of pupils who attend the school. One of the important ways that inclusive practice will move forward is if teachers listen to pupil and parent perspectives and are prepared to adopt flexible practices which take on board individual differences. Staff may require help in understanding how specific knowledge can reduce barriers to learning for pupils with disabilities. Often simple changes in classroom practices will help a broad range of pupils take a fuller part in the school curriculum and in school life.

Inclusion does not end with placement. For a pupil to feel included they should be able to take part socially and have friends. It will be very important for SENCos to listen to pupils' perspectives on their social well-being as well as monitoring academic progress. For example, pupils with disabilities may find making friends more difficult if they spend too much of their day with TAs. The peer group may tolerate the pupil with a disability, but not know how to fully include them in conversations or games. It may well be that part of a SENCo's role is to ensure that teachers and the peer group have training in disability issues so that ignorance does not produce attitudes which make real inclusion impossible. Each pupil is different and should have a say in how their learning is supported.

Building constructs

Everyone builds up their own construct of special needs or inclusion from their experience and knowledge, both personal and professional. My own research (Cowne 1993) demonstrated how constructs developed for course members as a result of attending courses and working on school-based practitioner research projects. SENCos and special needs teachers build up their confidence and competence by learning both the theory and practice of individual assessment and teaching, curriculum planning and differentiation, effective classroom management techniques and consultancy skills. Constructs grew in complexity as the teacher gained more experience and reflected on their own learning. Constructs were not fixed, although each individual had a core which was personal to them. It follows that the SENCo's role will also be built up from an interaction between his or her constructs and those of significant members of the school's staff. Each school will build its value systems, out of which all the policies, priorities and roles will develop.

It is only when SENCos are supported by heads and by, what one head called 'a critical number' of other staff, that change in the institution can occur. Head teachers' constructs of SEN are often different from their SENCo's. This may be because head teachers have other priorities, such as how well they are placed in the league tables. They often see SEN policy as helping to develop good classroom management and well-planned curriculum differentiation, resulting in better standards of teaching in their schools. SEN development therefore, becomes a lever for other school development. Indeed this is reflected at government level in professional development materials such as Leading on Inclusion (DfES 2005).

SENCos on training courses are often asked to develop an area of policy and practice for their course work. By engaging in reflective conversations, the SENCo can act as an agent of change, opening up opportunities for change management. *Developing Inclusive Practice: The SENCo's Role in Managing Change* (Cowne 2003) gives many practical examples of how SENCos on training courses have developed areas of school policy and practice.

Using this book to help manage your role as SENCo

Reviewing policy will include considering which tasks are to be performed by the SENCo along with other roles and responsibilities (see Chapter 2). Assessment and planning are important aspects of the role. There is a challenge when attempting to individualise support at the same time as diversifying resources to support a differentiated curriculum for all (see Chapters 3, 4 and 5). The inclusion of a wider range of pupils has resulted in more support personnel to manage and more multi-agency working (see Chapters 6 and 7). Tensions exist between wishing to use time to support pupils, parents and colleagues (the consultative role) and dealing with ever-increasing paperwork (the coordinating role) (see Chapters 8, 9 and 10).

This book has attempted to give practical advice, theoretical background and ideas to support SEN policy development and the SENCo's role within that development. Some readers will be experienced and for them I hope to have stimulated thought and challenged them to further reading. Others will have been more recently appointed and will need the detail the book provides. However, this book does not have all the answers. Some questions require local knowledge, some further research. SENCos will need to keep themselves informed about new government initiatives and documents, while being able to challenge and critique the thinking behind such publications. SENCos will have a significant role to play as long as they remain reflective practitioners, able to manage change in themselves, and hold meaningful conversations with colleagues, pupils and parents to develop the expertise and attitudes to make ordinary schools special places for all pupils.

Whole-school Policy for Special Educational Needs

Activity 1 Critical Incident Analysis

Activity 2 Audit of Whole-school Policy

Activity 3 Lesson Planning for Differentiation

Activity 4 Provision Mapping Exercise

Activity 5 Support Policy Review

Activity 6 Monitoring and Evaluation

Activity 1: Critical Incident Analysis

Managing change successfully

This activity can be used to explore participants' feelings when their role/expertise is challenged or they feel threatened in a professional context as a result of introducing a change in policy or practice. Example: a situation with one or more persons who are central to gaining acceptance for the new idea/policy practice. It is also a useful way of exploring and improving what is known as empathic listening skills.

Work in groups of three, giving each person a turn in each of the three roles.

- Person A relates their recently occurred critical incident (10 minutes).

- Person B listens and supports A's exploration of their thoughts and feelings.

- Person C observes the interaction between A and B and feeds back to the listener. The feedback is not about the incident, but about how the listener supported the teller (10 minutes) (see guidance note below). The observer also acts as time keeper for their group.

Guidelines for listener

Possible questions to ask:

- What was happening before/during the incident – how did you feel?

- If you could replay the incident, what would you have done differently/the same and why?

- What can you learn from those incidents about managing change within a system?

- What would you do next time such a situation arises?

- How could others assist?

These questions can lead to productive group discussion at the end of the session and time should be allocated for this because useful pointers can be elicited for the future.

Guidelines for observer

Note body posture, voice tone and non-verbal cues.
Note use of the following:

- *Open questions*: e.g. what thoughts and feelings did you have?

- *Reflective listening*: repeat a phrase

- *Selective reflection*: or select a phrase to repeat

- *Checking for understanding*

- *Empathic building*: e.g., it must have been difficult for you?

- *Summarising/taking stock*: e.g., let's review what choices you have.

Note also times when the listener's interactions became too invasive or instructive.

Activity 2: Audit of Whole-school Policy

Reviewing your whole-school policy for Special Educational Needs

The following exercise covers most aspects of a whole-school SEN policy. Select those that are most appropriate to your school. The aim is to give an opportunity for staff to discuss and reflect on what should be in the school's policy and how it is working at present. Areas for development and differing opinions may be revealed. These can be further explored in a discussion group.

If using this as a staff development exercise, individuals should work in small groups, such as year or curriculum teams, to reach some consensus of opinion on the most important priorities for the next year's work on the policy. This group activity starts by collating the group's individual results and looking for the biggest/smallest gap between the upper and lower line of markings.

Alternatively this audit could be given to staff as a questionnaire. The analysis of the data will provide information to the SENCo or the steering group.

Activity 2: Audit of whole-school policy – instructions

This checklist contains 16 statements about SEN policy or arrangements in schools. Its purpose is to help identify those points of your school's policy or arrangements in which there is scope for improvement. Each statement is followed by two lines – (a) and (b), for rating on a 1–5 scale.

Line (a) Ring the number which represents the extent to which you feel this **ought** to be in the whole-school policy on SEN: 1 = *must not be in*; 5 = *must be in.*

Line (b) Ring the number which represents your view of the **actual** situation at present: 1 = *not happening at all*; 5 = *happening completely.*

If you wish, add two more statements to cover any aspects not already mentioned. Rank these in the same way as the others. The difference between the ratings of the two lines may indicate the school's most important areas for action on the policy development. Discussion following this exercise within a staff or in-service meeting will serve as a way to reach consensus over priorities for the next year (concept developed from Evans *et al.* 1981).

1 There is an operational policy for SEN which has principles consistent with the Code of Practice (2001) and SENDA.
(a) 1   2   3   4   5
(b) 1   2   3   4   5

2 The key principles of the schools SEN policy are known to all staff.
(a) 1   2   3   4   5
(b) 1   2   3   4   5

3 There are descriptive guidelines of the roles and responsibilities of staff in relation to SEN. These include roles for governors, head, SENCos, teachers and TAs.
(a) 1   2   3   4   5
(b) 1   2   3   4   5

4 Arrangements for assessing pupils' progress are part of whole-school assessment practice.
(a) 1   2   3   4   5
(b) 1   2   3   4   5

5 There are arrangements in place to organise regular reviews of progress for all pupils with SEN.
(a) 1   2   3   4   5
(b) 1   2   3   4   5

6 Pupils are involved in decision-making during the planning of their provision.
(a) 1   2   3   4   5
(b) 1   2   3   4   5

7 Staff are supported in the development of a range of teaching strategies, learning activities and support materials which enhance the access to the curriculum for pupils with SEN.
(a) 1   2   3   4   5
(b) 1   2   3   4   5

8   Planning for pupils with SEN is an integral part of general curriculum planning.
    (a) 1   2   3   4   5
    (b) 1   2   3   4   5

9   There is a staff development policy for SEN which relates to the school improvement plan and reflects both school and individual priorities and needs.
    (a) 1   2   3   4   5
    (b) 1   2   3   4   5

10 Parents are involved in the planning of future provision for their child's additional needs.
    (a) 1   2   3   4   5
    (b) 1   2   3   4   5

11 Parents are given information about the school's policy and procedures for SEN.
    (a) 1   2   3   4   5
    (b) 1   2   3   4   5

12 Support staff have clear roles and are encouraged to work as members of a team to enhance inclusive practice.
    (a) 1   2   3   4   5
    (b) 1   2   3   4   5

13 Liaison time is available for class or subject teachers to plan effectively with support staff.
    (a) 1   2   3   4   5
    (b) 1   2   3   4   5

14 The school's rational for allocating resources for SEN are clearly described and understood by all staff.
    (a) 1   2   3   4   5
    (b) 1   2   3   4   5

15 There are clear procedures known to relevant staff for making referrals to outside agencies.
    (a) 1   2   3   4   5
    (b) 1   2   3   4   5

16 Disabled pupils have access to all aspects of school life including extended school activities.
    (a) 1   2   3   4   5
    (b) 1   2   3   4   5

Activity 3: Lesson Planning for Differentiation

1   Choose a topic within your subject.

2   Answer questions 1 and 2.

3   Define learning outcomes for the lesson.
    What should the pupils learn? (Give range of outcomes if necessary.)

4   What different assessment modalities (such as oral, written, demonstration) will be used?

5   Write down prerequisite baseline skills or concepts that you are assuming to present in the class, before you start. (Change boxes to suit yourself.)

6   Think of up to three pupils with additional/significant needs. List the barriers to learning that this topic might produce for these children.

7   If staff development time allows, discuss continuity and cross-curricular issues. What should have been covered by previous lessons or in other subjects? Will this cause confusion to students? Are there 'bridging' needs to cross-reference between subjects?

8   Decide if any modifications to your planning are necessary in the light of this discussion.

9   Add extension ideas for your more able pupils.

Activity 3: Differentiation exercise for Key Stage 1 and 2 lessons

Question 1:
Is this realistic to do in the time allocated?

Question 2:
Is this relevant to this group of students?

Topic		Extension
Core curriculum objectives		
Strategies/methods/resources		
How will outcomes be assessed?		

Modification		

Pre-requisite baseline skills

Language skills (written)	Social skills	Key concepts needed
Number skills	Organisational skills	

Language skills (oral)		
Manipulative		

Activity 3: Differentiation exercise for a Key Stage 3 lesson

Question 1:
Is this realistic to do in the time allocated?

Question 2:
Is this relevant to this group of students?

Topic		Extension
Core curriculum objectives e.g. tasks, skills, concepts		
Delivery methods/resources/support		
How will outcomes be assessed?		
Modification		

Pre-requisite baseline skills

Linguistic	Social	Organisational	Subject specific
Numerical	Thinking	Other	

© Elizabeth Cowne, 2008

Activity 4: Provision Mapping Exercise

This activity will support you in starting a provision map for your school. Provision mapping is an 'at a glance' way of showing all the provision a school makes, identifying needs and staff skills required to meet those needs. Costs can be calculated which enable schools to track their SEN spending. This complete picture allows schools to see the impact of their interventions, identify gaps in provision and when linked with assessment, can show the progress pupils make. Interventions will be those that are *additional to* and *different from* the school's differentiated curriculum. The process of provision mapping is the responsibility of the whole school, not just the SENCo.

Step 1
There are choices about the first stage of provision mapping. The principle behind this first stage is to gather information about which children have additional /different needs, and what these needs are.

One way to start is to use a *must/should/could* sheet to gather information about pupil needs across each year group. Along the top of the sheet are listed all the interventions that are currently available, with spare columns for any additions. In the rows down, teachers name pupils who 'must' have an intervention, those that 'should' and those who 'would benefit from' (*could*) an intervention. Pupils with statements and those with clearly identified needs at SAP are likely to be listed in the *must* rows; those on SA in the *should* row others for whom there is a concern in the *could* row. If pupils require interventions that are not listed, they can be added along the top row.

Note: It is not necessary to list provision provided for Wave 1 or 2 of the Literacy/Numeracy strategies (see *Leading on Inclusion*, DfES 2005).

Step 2
Collect all the information you have gathered and check any variations from your SEN profile, any gaps in provision and number of hours available for each intervention.

Step 3
It is important that you have evidence to show that your choice of interventions work and enable pupils to make progress.

Step 4
Assess if staff have adequate training to carry out interventions.

Step 5
At this point it is useful to identify the funding available for SEN. Resources allocated to pupils are the direct interventions with pupils,and resources allocated amongst, are those that are required to keep the SEN machine running smoothly. Cost your provision map. Include only those interventions that are additional to or different from what is normally available to all pupils. Use average costs for staffing. This is an accountability exercise not an accounting one! Only that part of the SENCo salary that is direct work with children should be part of the provision map costs

Step 6
Draw up a provision map for each year group using the information you have gathered and share the big picture with staff.

Step 7
Evaluating the impact of your provision is essential. This can be done by measuring pupil outcomes through National Curriculum levels, use of P scales and progress towards whole school target setting for different pupil groups. It is also important to include pupils and parents views in your evaluation as well as teachers views. Review your map on an annual basis. You may want to do this in the summer term, in preparation for the new academic year.

(Adapted from Hrekow 2006: *Provision Mapping/Management materials*, SENJIT.)

Activity 4: Provision mapping exercise

The following forms could be completed by participants in a training group of SENCos (or others). List ways in which support is currently being used in each year group, or extract and collate the provision information from the IEPs, GEPs and statements. Below is a list of potential examples of types of support. You may want to add other activities applicable to your school.

Primary
- speech and language activities as set up by the therapist
- daily speaking and listening groups
- mathematics extension, e.g. 'Springboard' or support
- small group work for literacy/numeracy
- circle of friends activities
- circle time
- extra time using ICT with support
- counselling group
- individual in-class support for target achievement
- Reading Recovery programmes
- home-school book-bags/diaries
- nurture group placement
- phonological awareness programme
- paired reading
- social skills groups
- behaviour management.

Secondary
- circle of friends activities
- extra time using ICT with support
- counselling group/individual
- individual/group support for achieving targets
- paired reading
- touch typing
- 'buddy' system organisation
- study skills
- anger management group
- behaviour management programme
- support option: Key Stage 4.

Activity 4: Provision mapping exercise

	P r i m a r y			
Year Group	**Provision/resource for groups/individuals**	**Staff involved**	**Staff ratio**	**Cost** (SENCo may need help from SMT for this)
Nursery	✧			
Reception	✧			
Year 1/2	✧			
Year 3/4	✧			
Year 5/6	✧			

Activity 4: Provision mapping exercise

— — S e c o n d a r y — —				
Year Group	**Provision/resource for groups/individuals**	**Staff involved**	**Staff ratio**	**Cost** (SENCo may need help from SMT for this)
Year 7	✧			
Year 8	✧			
Year 9	✧			
Year 10	✧			
Year 11	✧			

Activity 5: Support Policy Review

Reviewing your policy for managing support. You are asked to mark the following statements on a scale of 1–5.

Line (a) According to your **ideal** view: 1 = *not necessary*; 5 = *highly necessary*
Line (b) According to how you view **actual** practice at the moment: 1 = *not happening at all*; 5 = *happening well*

Using the statements given below, mark your, (a) ideal, and (b) actual practice ratings.

1   Teaching Assistants (TAs)/support staff have clearly written job descriptions provided when they start their job in the school.
   (a) 1   2   3   4   5
   (b) 1   2   3   4   5

2   TAs have useful induction training when they start their job in the school.
   (a) 1   2   3   4   5
   (b) 1   2   3   4   5

3   TAs/support staff are managed by the SENCo or a member of SMT.
   (a) 1   2   3   4   5
   (b) 1   2   3   4   5

4   TAs have regular meetings with their class/subject teachers to plan lessons.
   (a) 1   2   3   4   5
   (b) 1   2   3   4   5

5   TAs have some timetabled time for relevant preparation, meetings and record keeping.
   (a) 1   2   3   4   5
   (b) 1   2   3   4   5

6   TAs have a clear understanding of their role as part of a team; supporting teachers to support the pupils.
   (a) 1   2   3   4   5
   (b) 1   2   3   4   5

7   TAs encourage pupils to develop independence and to preserve their autonomy.
   (a) 1   2   3   4   5
   (b) 1   2   3   4   5

8   TAs promote peer group acceptance and inclusion.
   (a) 1   2   3   4   5
   (b) 1   2   3   4   5

9 TAs use supportive language when working with pupils.
   (a) 1   2   3   4   5
   (b) 1   2   3   4   5

10 TAs follow procedures when the class teacher is absent.
   (a) 1   2   3   4   5
   (b) 1   2   3   4   5

11 Support staff follow safe guarding of child protection issues and procedures.
   (a) 1   2   3   4   5
   (b) 1   2   3   4   5

12 TAs' skills and expertise in particular areas of the curriculum are recognised and used in those subject areas.
   (a) 1   2   3   4   5
   (b) 1   2   3   4   5

13 TAs share their skills and expertise in managing different types of LDDs.
   (a) 1   2   3   4   5
   (b) 1   2   3   4   5

14 TAs are given lesson plans and medium-term plans, as appropriate.
   (a) 1   2   3   4   5
   (b) 1   2   3   4   5

15 TAs are trained in effective behaviour management techniques.
   (a) 1   2   3   4   5
   (b) 1   2   3   4   5

16 TAs have regular meetings as a team and /or with their line manager.
   (a) 1   2   3   4   5
   (b) 1   2   3   4   5

Now, write your own additional sentence(s) to cover aspects of the policy and practice not covered above. Rate these in the same way on an (a) and (b) line.

Activity 6: Monitoring and Evaluation

(Adapted from the Special Educational Needs Joint Initiative for Training (SENJIT) School Special Educational Needs Policies Pack Unit 13: NCB/SENJIT 2005.)

Monitoring and evaluating a school's policy will be informed first of all by the values and principles which underpin the SEN/Inclusion policy and practice. Choice of aspects to monitor and evaluate will be led by the current self-evaluation in relation to SIP. The SENCo will play an important role in keeping issues on the agenda but should be aware of how to integrate those with other priorities. The aim of the school's SEN policy will be to improve the way it enables pupils to learn and progress, so it will be critical to take account of the outcomes for SEN pupils. Use existing information from:

- self-evaluation data
- Ofsted comments
- pupil records
- attendance and exclusion data
- provision mapping data in funding given and provision planned.

Steps

1 Choose priority areas for development
2 Collect existing data relevant to this area
3 Draw on views of teachers, TAs, parents and pupils
4 Decide on:
    - targets and success criteria (see notes below)
    - who will be actively responsible for parts of the work, the role governors will play, how all staff will be involved, how will pupils and parents/carers be informed and involved
    - dates when certain activities will take place or be completed
    - the success criteria or performance indicators.
5 How progress will be monitored and judgements made.

Performance indicators or success criteria?

A performance indicator can be expressed in numerical terms such as a percentage or by effectiveness expressed as a judgement, or by a mixture of both methods. But the purpose remains the same, which is to answer the question – how will we know how we are doing?

Sometimes it is sufficient to note that an event took place: e.g., a meeting was held. At other times a longer-term success criteria is required which can be sustained over a period of time and then evaluated. Evaluation includes making a value judgement about how effective an action was and from whose perspectives. The sample sheet below shows how these steps could be planned and mapped for easy interpretation. Working an example using each column will help the SENCo and others to see clearly what might be needed.

Activity 6: Action plan and success criteria

Aim	Action	By when	By whom	Techniques	Success criteria	M&E

Notes

- *Aim* – In this column list up to four aims connected to your chosen area of policy/practice development. These will have arisen from initial consultations, audit analysis, and are likely to form part of the school's improvement plan.
- *Action*: state what will be done, e.g. consultation, in-service, meeting, induction pack, initiate a change in practice, or develop a written policy.
- *By when and by whom*: give dates and roles.
- *Techniques*: i.e. interview, questionnaire, data analysis, consultation meeting.
- *Success criteria*: qualitative, quantitative (see page above).
- *M&E – monitoring*: state who will monitor the progress of your plan. Evaluation – judgements as to whether the success criteria are reached and are valuable to the relevant people.

Source Lists

Source List 1a: Assessment Materials

(Unless otherwise stated all material is published by NFER/Nelson, Slough. Tel: 0845 602 1937. Website: nfer/nelson.co.uk)

Early years

Cameron, R. J. and White, M. (1987) *Portage Early Education Programme.* 0–6 years.
Clay, M. (1985) *Sand: 'Concepts about Print', Tests*, Beginning Readers. Oxford: Heinemann.
Downing, J., Schaefer, B. and Ayres, J. D. (1994) *Larr Test of Emergent Literacy.* 4–5.3 years.
Lindsay, G. and Desforges, M. (1998) *Baseline Assessment: Practice, problems and possibilities.* London: David Fulton Publishers.
Pearson, L. and Quinn, J. (1980) *Bury Infant Checklist.* A development checklist for 5-year-olds.

Tests of general ability

Dunn, L., Dunn, L. M., Whetton, C. and Burley, J. (1997) *British Picture Vocabulary Scale*, 2nd edn. 3–15.8 years.
Raven, J. C. (1998) *Raven's Progressive Matrices and Vocabulary Scales.* Three levels available.

Screening programmes

Robertson, A., Robertson, A., Henderson, A., Fisher, J. and Gibson, M. (1995) *Quest: Identifying children with reading and writing difficulties*, 2nd edn. 6–8 years+.

Reading tests: individual

Bookbinder, G. (2002) *Salford Sentence Reading Test*, revised. 6–10.5 years. London: Hodder and Stoughton.
Miller-Guron, L. (1999) *Wordchains.* Word reading screening test.
Neale, M. (1997) *Neale Analysis of Reading Ability*, 2nd edn, revised. 6–13 years.
Vincent, D., De la Mare, M. and Arnold, H. (1990) *Individual Reading Analysis.* 5/6–11 years.

Material for miscue analysis

Crumpler, M. and McCarty, C. (2004) *Diagnostic Reading Analysis: 7–16 years.* London: Hodder and Stoughton.

Source List 1b: Further Reading

Assessment

Black, P. and Wiliam, D. (2002) *Working Inside the Black Box: Assessment for learning in the classroom.* London: Kings College.
Clarke, S. (2005) *Formative Assessment in the Secondary Classroom.* London: Hodder and Stoughton.

IEP software

Csars software. *CSARS*. www.csars.co.uk
Learn How Publications. *IEP Writer 2*. www.iepwriter.co.uk
Modbury Group. *Enable Software*. www.enable-online.com
SEMERC/Granada Learning. *IEP Manager*. www.granada-learning.com

Performance (P) scales

Planning, Teaching and Assessing the Curriculum for Pupils with Learning Difficulties, DfEE/QCA (2001)
www.bsquared.co.uk/index.php
www.lancashire.gov.uk/education/pivots/

Curriculum

Byers, R. and Rose, R. (2004) *Planning the Curriculum for Pupils with SEN: A practical Guide*, 2nd edn. London: David Fulton Publishers.
Edwards, S. (2007) *Primary Mathematics for Teaching Assistants*. London: Fulton/Routledge.
Feasey, R. (2007) *Primary Science for Teaching Assistants*. London: Fulton/Routledge.
Galloway, J. (2007) *Primary ICT for Teaching Assistants*. London: Fulton/Routledge.
Grove, N. (1998) *Literature for All: Developing literature in the curriculum for pupils with special educational needs*. London: David Fulton Publishers.
McKeown, S. (2004) *Meeting SEN in the Curriculum: Modern foreign languages*. London: David Fulton Publishers.
Roffey, S. (2006) *Circle Time for Emotional Literacy*. London: Paul Chapman Publishing.
Tilstone, C., Lacey, P., Porter, J. and Robertson, C. (2000) *Pupils with Learning Difficulties in Mainstream Schools*. London: David Fulton Publishers.

Literacy and Numeracy

Berger, A. and Gross, J. (1999) *Teaching the Literacy Hour in an Inclusive Classroom: Supporting pupils with learning difficulties in a mainstream environment*. London: David Fulton Publishers.
Berger, A., Denise, M. and Portman, J. (2000) *Implementing the National Numeracy Strategy for Pupils with Learning Difficulties: Access to the daily mathematics lesson*. London: David Fulton Publishers.
Fox, G. and Halliwell, M. (2000) *Supporting Literacy and Numeracy: A guide for LSAs*. London: David Fulton Publishers.
Henderson, A. (1998) *Maths for the Dyslexic: A practical guide*. London: David Fulton Publishers.
Hinson, M. (ed.) (1999) *Surviving the Literacy Hour*. Stafford: National Association of Special Educational Needs (NASEN).
Morfett, C., edited by Higgs, J. and Gray, G. (1999) *Mathematics Assessment Pack*. London: SENSS, London Borough of Croydon.
National Literacy and Number Strategies, The (2002) *Including All Children in the Literacy Hour and Daily Mathematics Lesson*. DfES 0465/2002.
Pollock, J. and Waller, E. (1997) *Day-to-day Dyslexia in the Classroom*. London: Routledge.
Reason, R. and Boote, R. (1994) *Helping Children with Reading and Spelling: A special needs manual*. London: Routledge.
Sassoon, R. (2003) *Handwriting: The way to teach it*, 2nd edn. London: Paul Chapman Publishing.

Thinking skills

Lipman, M., Sharp, M. and Oscanyan, F. (1980) *Philosophy in the Classroom*. Philadelphia: Temple University Press.
Smith, A. (1996) *Accelerated Learning in the Classroom*. Stafford: Network Educational Press Ltd.
Wallace, B. (ed.) (2001) *Teaching Thinking Skills across the Primary Curriculum: A practical approach for all abilities*. London: David Fulton Publishers.

Social, emotional and behavioural difficulties

Bayley, J. and Haddock, L. (1999) *Training Teachers in Behavioural Management*. London: SENJIT.

Kingston Friends Workshop Group and Anne Rawlings (1996) *Ways and Means Today*. Kingston: KFWG.

Long, R. (2007) *Omnibus Edition of Better Behaviour*. London: Routledge.

Ripley, K. and Simpson, E. (2007) *First Steps to Emotional Literacy*. London: Fulton/Routledge.

Rogers, B. (2000) *Classroom Behaviour: A practical guide to effective teaching, behaviour management and colleague support*. London: Books Education.

Watkins, O. and Wagner, R. (2000) *Improving School Behaviour*. London: Paul Chapman.

Disability information

Farrell, M. (2006) *Moderate, Severe and Profound Learning Difficulties*. London: David Fulton Publishers.

Hardy, C., Ogden, J., Newman, J. and Cooper, S. (2002) *Autism and ICT: A Guide for Teachers and Parents*. London: David Fulton Publishers.

Hull Learning Series (2004) *Supporting Children with Speech and Language Difficulties*. London: David Fulton Publishers.

Hull Learning Series (2004) *Supporting Children with Epilepsy*. London: David Fulton Publishers.

Hull Learning Series (2006) *Supporting Children with Autistic Spectrum Disorder*. London: Routledge.

Kewley, G. (2005) *Attention Deficit Hyperactivity Disorder: What can teachers do?*, 2nd edn. London: David Fulton Publishers.

Lee, M. G. (2004) *Co-ordination Difficulties: Practical ways forward*. London: David Fulton Publishers.

Pickles, P. (2004) *Managing the Curriculum for Children with Severe Motor Difficulties*. London: David Fulton Publishers.

Riddick, B., Wolfe, J. and Lumsden, D. (2006) *Dyslexia: A practical guide for teachers and parents*. London: David Fulton Publishers.

Salisbury, R. (ed.) (2008) *Teaching Pupils with Visual Impairment: A guide to making the school curriculum accessible*. London: Routledge.

Saunders, S. (2001) *Fragile X Syndrome: A guide for teachers*. London: David Fulton Publishers.

Inclusion

Briggs, S. (2005) *Inclusion and How to Do It*. London: David Fulton Publishers.

Ofsted (2004) *Special Educational Needs and Disability: Towards inclusive schools*. HMI 2276.

Reed, G. (2005) *Learning Styles and Inclusion*. London: Paul Chapman Publishing.

Person-centred planning

www.helensandersonassociates.co.uk

www.secondary.newham.gov.uk

Policy making

Advisory Centre for Education (ACE) (2005) *Special Education Handbook*, 9th edn. London: ACE, www.ace-ed.org.uk

Audit Commission/ESTYN/Ofsted (2001) *Managing Special Educational Needs: A self-review handbook for local educational authorities*. Audit Commission, www.audit-commission.gov.uk

Fullan, M. (1999) *Change Forces: The sequel*. London: Falmer Press.

Swzed, C. (2007) 'Reconsidering the role of the primary Special Educational Needs Coordinator: policy practice and future priorities', *British Journal of Special Education*, 34(2), 96–104.

Teaching assistants

Balshaw, M. Farrell, P (2002) *Teaching Assistants: Practical strategies for effective support.* London: David Fulton Publishers.
Birkett, V. (2004) *How to Support and Manage TAs.* London: LDA.

Further education

Grove, B. and Saunders, G. (2003) 'Connecting with connexions: the role of the personal adviser with young people with special educational and support needs, *Support for Learning*, 18(1), 12–17.
Maudslay, L. (2003) 'Policy changes in post-school learning for people with disabilities and learning difficulties and the implications for practice', *Support for Learning*, 18(1), 6–11.

Journals

Special children

Questions Publishing Company, www.teachingtimes.co.uk

British Journal of Support for Learning

NASEN Publications, www.nasen.org.uk

British Journal of Special Education

NASEN Publications, www.nasen.org.uk

SENCo Forum

To join, go to: http: *lists.becta.org.uk/mailman/listinfo/senco-forum*
Further info.: Terry Waller, BECTA, Milburn Hill Rd, Science Park, Coventry, CV4 7JJ. Tel: 02476 416994

SENCo Update

(Monthly publication which informs SENCos of recent government documents and initiatives.)
Optimus Publishing, www.optimuspub.co.uk

Source List 2: Voluntary Organisations

ACE Centre Advisory Trust

www.ace-centre.org.uk
Tel: 01865 759800
92 Windmill Road, Headington, Oxford, OX3 7DR

Advisory Centre for Education (ACE) Ltd

www.ace-ed.org.uk
Exclusion infoline (24hr): 020 7704 9822
Adviceline: 0808 800 5793 (M–F, 10–5 p.m.)
Admin. Tel: 020 7704 3370 (M–F, 9.30–5.30 p.m.)
Unit 1c, Aberdeen Studios, 22 Highbury Grove, London, N5 2DQ

Association for all Speech Impaired Children (AFASIC)

www.afasic.org.uk
Helpline: 0845 355 5577 (M–F, 10.30–2.30 p.m.)
Admin. Tel: 020 7490 9410
Second Floor, 50–52 Great Sutton Street, London, EC1V ODJ

British Dyslexia Association

www.bda-dyslexia.org.uk
Helpline: 0118 966 8271
98 London Road, Reading, Berkshire, RG1 5AU

Contact-a-Family

www.cafamily.org.uk
Helpline: 0808 808 3555 (M–F, 10–4 p.m.; M, 5.30–7.30 p.m.)
Textphone: 0808 808 3556
209–211 City Road, London, EC1V 1JN

Council for Disabled Children

website: www.ncb.org.uk
Tel: 020 7843 1900
c/o National Children's Bureau, 8 Wakley Street, London, EC1V 7QE

CSIE (Centre for Studies on Inclusive Education)

www.csie.org.uk
Tel: 0117 328 4007
New Redland Building, Coldharbour Lane, Frenchay, Bristol, BS16 1QU

Cystic Fibrosis Trust

www.cftrust.org.uk
Tel: 020 8464 7211
11 London Road, Bromley, Kent, BR1 1BY

Disability Alliance

www.disabilityalliance.org
Tel: 020 7247 8776
[Authors of the *Disability Rights Handbook*]
Universal House, 88–94 Wentworth Street, London, E1 7SA

Disability Rights Commission

www.drc-gb.org
Textphone: 08457 622644
Tel: 08457 622633

Disabled Living Foundation

www.dlf.org.uk
Helpline: 0845 130 9177 (M–F, 10–4 p.m.)
Tel: 020 7289 6111
380–384 Harrow Road, London, W9 2HU

Down's Syndrome Association (DSA)

www.downs-syndrome.org.uk
Helpline: 0845 230 0372 (M–F, 10–4 p.m.)
Langdon Down Centre, 2a Langdon Park, Teddington, Middx, TW11 9PS

Epilepsy Action (British Epilepsy Association)

www.epilepsy.org.uk
Helpline: 0808 800 5050 (M–Th 9–4.30 p.m.; F, 9–4 p.m.)
International: 0113 210 8800
New Anstey House, Gate Way Drive, Yeadon, Leeds, LS19 7XY

Independent Panel for Special Education Advice (IPSEA)

www.ipsea.org.uk
Adviceline: 0800 0184016
General Enquiries: 01394 384711
Carlow Mews, Woodbridge, Suffolk, IP12 1EA

Invalid Children's Aid Nationwide (ICAN)

www.ican.org.uk
Tel: 0845 2254071
8 Wakley St, London, EC1V 7QE

MENCAP

www.mencap.org.uk
Tel: 020 7454 0454
123 Golden Lane, London, EC1Y ORT

MIND

www.mind.org.uk
Mind*info*line: 0845 766 0163 (M–F, 9.15–5.15 p.m.)
Tel: 020 8519 2122
15–19 Broadway, London, E15 4BQ

National Association of Special Educational Needs (NASEN)

www.nasen.org.uk
Tel: 01827 311500
Membership Department and Publications:
NASEN House, 4/5 Amber Business Village, Amber Close, Amington, Tamworth, Staffs,
B77 4RP

National Association of Toy and Leisure Libraries

www.natll.org.uk
Tel: 0207 255 4600
68 Churchway, London, NW1 1LT

National Autistic Society

www.nas.org.uk
Helpline: 0845 070 4004
Tel: 020 7833 2299
393 City Road, London, EC1V 1NG

National Deaf Children's Society (NDCS)

www.ndcs.org.uk
Tel: 0808 800 8880; 020 7490 8656
15 Dufferin Street, London, EC1Y SUR

National Institute of Conductive Education

The Foundation for Conductive Education
www.conductive-education.org.uk
Tel: 0121 449 1569
Cannon Hill House, Russell Road, Birmingham, B13 8RD

Network 81

www.network81.org
Tel: 0870 770 3306
Admin. Tel: 0870 770 3262
1–7 Woodfield Terrace, Chapel Hill, Stansted, Essex, CM24 8AJ
[Parent support organisation – helpline, befrienders]

Parents for Inclusion

www.parentsforinclusion.org.uk
Helpline: 0800 652 3145 (M–Th, 10–12 & 1–3 p.m.)
Admin.: Tel: 020 7735 7735
Winchester House, Kennington Park Business Estate, Cranmer Rd, London, SW9 6EJ

Royal Association for Disability and Rehabilitation (RADAR)

www.radar.org.uk
Tel: 020 7250 3222
12 City Forum, 250 City Road, London, EC1V 8AF

Royal National Institute for the Blind (RNIB)

www.rnib.org.uk
Helpline: 0845 766 9999 (M–F, 9–5 p.m.; W, 9–4)
Tel: 020 7388 1266
105 Judd Street, London, WC1H 9NE

Royal National Institute for the Deaf (RNID)

www.rnid.org.uk
Freephone: 0808 808 0123
Textphone: 0808 808 9000
19–23 Featherstone Street, London, EC1Y 8SL

SCOPE

www.scope.org.uk
Tel: 020 7619 7100
Scope Response: 0808 800 3333 (M–F, 9–7 p.m.; Sat, 10–2 p.m.)
6 Market Rd, London, N7 9PW

SENSE (UK deaf/blind charity)

www.sense.org.uk
Tel: 0845 127 006
11–13 Clifton Terrace, Finsbury Park, London, N4 3SR

SKILL (National Bureau for Students with Disabilities)

www.skill.org.uk
Infoline: 0800 328 5050
Minicom: 0800 068 2422
HO: Chapter House, 18–20 Crucifix Lane, London, SE1 3JW

Appendices

Note: The appendices are numbered as they relate to the chapters.

Appendix 1a: Categories of disability used by LEAs (1959)

These were listed as:

a) blind pupils – pupils whose sight is so defective they require education by methods not using sight.
b) partially sighted pupils – educated by special methods involving use of sight.
c) deaf pupils.
d) partially hearing pupils.
e) educationally subnormal pupils.
f) epileptic pupils – pupils who by reason of epilepsy cannot be educated under a normal regime.
g) maladjusted pupils – emotional instability or disturbance.
h) physically handicapped pupils.
i) pupils suffering from speech defect.
j) delicate pupils – pupils not falling under any other category who need a change of environment and who cannot without risk to health or educational development be educated under a normal regime of an ordinary school.

(Handicapped Pupils and Special Schools Regulation 1959)

The largest category of children requiring special education was those described as 'educationally subnormal' (ESN). These were children who were backward in basic subjects as well as those who were seen as 'dull'. Pupils with severe learning difficulties were not educated in schools at this time.

Appendix 1b: Categories of need used in Code of Practice (2001)

The Code of Practice uses the following categories to define needs.
Children will have needs and requirements which may fall into at least one of four areas; many children will have inter-related needs. The impact of these combinations on the child's ability to function, learn and succeed should be taken into account.'

(Code of Practice, DfES 2001b: 7.52)

The areas of need to be recorded for the Pupil Level Annual Schools Census (PLASC) are:

a) Cognition and Learning Needs
   Specific Learning Difficulty (SpLD)
   Moderate Learning Difficulty (MLD)
   Severe Learning Difficulty (SLD)
   Profound and Multiple Learning Difficulty (PMLD)
b) Behaviour, Emotional and Social Development Needs (BESD)

c) Communication and Interaction Needs
   Speech, Language and Communication Needs (SLCN)
   Autistic Spectrum Disorder (ASD)
d) Sensory and/or Physical Needs
   Visual Impairment (VI)
   Hearing Impairment (HI)
   Multi-Sensory Impairment (MSI)
   Physical Disability (PD)

Details of the types of provision likely to be required for each of these categories is given in the Code of Practice paragraphs 7.55–7.67.

Appendix 1c: Definition of disability

Note: This is a wider definition then those used for SEN

A person has a disability if he or she has a physical or mental impairment, which has a substantial and long-term adverse effect on his or her ability to carry out normal day-to-day activities. 'Impairment' can be physical or mental. This includes sensory impairments, such as those affecting sight or hearing. The term 'mental impairment' is intended to cover a wide range of impairments relating to mental functioning, including what are often known as learning disabilities.

(*The Duty to Promote Disability Equality: Statutory Code of Practice*, TSO 2005)

Appendix 2a: Schedule 1: Regulation 3 (1)

Basic information about the school's special educational provision

1. The objectives of the governing body in making provision for pupils with special educational needs, and a description of how the governing body's special educational needs policy will contribute towards meeting those objectives.
2. The name of the person who is responsible for co-ordinating the day-to-day provision of education for pupils with special educational needs at the school (whether or not the person is known as the SENCo).
3. The arrangements which have been made for coordinating the provision of education for pupils with special educational needs at the school.
4. The admission arrangements for pupils with special educational needs who do not have a statement in so far as they differ from the arrangements for other pupils.
5. The kinds of provision for special educational needs in which the school specialises and any special units.
6. Facilities for pupils with special educational needs at the school including facilities which increase or assist access to the school by pupils who are disabled.

Information about the school's policies for the identification and assessment of, and provision for, all pupils with Special Educational Needs

7. How resources are allocated to and among pupils with special educational needs.
8. How pupils with special educational needs are identified and their needs determined and reviewed.
9. Arrangements for providing access by pupils with special educational needs to a balanced and broadly based curriculum (including the National Curriculum).
10. How pupils with special educational needs engage in the activities of the school together with pupils who do not have special educational needs.
11. How the governing body evaluates the success of the education which is provided at the school to pupils with special educational needs.
12. Any arrangements made by the governing body relating to the treatment of complaints from parents of pupils with special educational needs concerning the provision made at the school.

Information about the school's staffing policies and partnership with bodies beyond the school

13. Any arrangements made by the governing body relating to in-service training for staff in relation to special educational needs.
14. The use made of teachers and facilities from outside the school, including links with support services for special educational needs.
15. The role played by the parents of pupils with special educational needs.
16. Any links with other schools, including special schools, and the provision made for the transition of pupils with special educational needs between schools or between the school and the next stage of life or education.
17. Links with child health services, social services and educational welfare services, and any voluntary organisations which work on behalf of children with special educational needs.

The Education (Special Educational Needs – Information) (England) Regulations 1999. Code of Practice (2001)

Appendix 2b: Governors' responsibilities

The governing body must:

- do their best to secure that the necessary provision is made for any pupil who has SEN;
- ensure that, where the 'responsible person' – the head teacher or the appropriate governor – has been informed by the LEA that a pupil has SEN, those needs are known to all who are likely to teach him or her;
- secure that teachers in the school are aware of the importance of identifying, and providing for, those pupils who have SEN;
- consult the LEA; as appropriate, the Funding Authority; and the governing bodies of other schools, when it seems to them necessary or desirable in the interests of coordinated special educational provision in the area as a whole;
- report annually to parents on the school's policy for pupils with SEN;
- ensure that the pupil joins in the activities of the school together with pupils who do not have SEN, so far as that is reasonably practical and compatible with the pupil receiving the necessary special educational provision, the efficient education of other children in the school and the efficient use of resources;
- have regard to the Code of Practice when carrying out their duties towards pupils with SEN.

(Education Act 1996, Sections 313, 317A)

Appendix 3: The relationship between bilingual learners' language stages and Code of Practice stages

Bilingual learners are often classified by EAL teachers by their stages of development in learning English. This should not be confused with the Code of Practice graduated response.

Bilingual stages

- *Stage 1*: new to English
- *Stage 2*: learning familiarity with English
- *Stage 3*: becoming confident in use of English
- *Stage 4*: on the way to fluent use of English in most social learning contexts.

Things to do

- Find out how long the pupil has been learning English.
- Talk to parents about the child in the home context and what language(s) are spoken at home.
- Check health records and previous educational history.
- More information in *Assessing the Needs of Bilingual Pupils*, by Hall 2001.

Pupils at bilingual Stage 1 should not be given an IEP unless they have clearly identified LDD. Pupils at bilingual Stage 1 will often be supported by teachers from a bilingual service (EMAG). It takes up to two years to develop basic interpersonal communication. EMAG teachers can give advice on how to support and teach these pupils to acquire their new language while retaining the use of their own first language.

Appendix 4: Instrumental Enrichment: cognitive functions as expressed by students

Input: gathering all the information we need

- using senses to gather clear and complete information
- using a plan so we don't miss anything
- giving all of this a name so we can talk about it
- describing things in terms of where and when they occur
- deciding on characteristics which stay the same
- organising the information we gather by considering more than one thing at a time
- being precise and accurate when it matters.

Elaboration: using the information we have gathered

- defining a problem, what we must do and what we must figure out
- using only that part of the information that is relevant
- having a picture in our mind of what we are looking for and what we aim to do
- making a plan which will involve steps needed to reach our goal
- remembering various pieces of information we will need
- looking for relationships
- comparing objects or experiences
- finding categories or sets
- thinking about 'what if' questions
- using logic to defend out opinions.

Output: expressing the solution to a problem

- being clear and precise so you can be understood
- thinking things through before you answer and waiting before you say something you may regret
- not panicking if you cannot immediately answer a question, return to it later.
- carrying a picture in your mind for comparison without losing or changing details.

(Adapted from Adey and Shayer 1994)

Feuerstein *et al.* (1980) lists the nature and focus of cognitive impairments related to his three phases of information processing: Input, Elaboration and Output. These include lack of planning, impulsive behaviour, impaired receptive verbal tools, impaired spatial orientation or temporal concepts, inability to define a problem or pursue logical evidence. It is his programme of instrumental enrichment which is designed to overcome these impaired processes and blocked learning.

Appendix 6: Advice on how teaching assistants can support the needs of different types of SEN

(For more detail, see TDA 2006, *Teaching Assistant File*.)

Physical difficulties (e.g. Cerebral Palsy)

The TA's main aim will be to enable the pupil to be as independent as possible. It can be a complex role supporting those with severe physical disabilities. It is likely to involve carrying out physiotherapy, occupational therapy and possibly speech and language therapy under the guidance of visiting therapists. These programmes are carried out by assistants to improve the child's physical mobility and communication skills. TAs may require training in the use of technical aids and ICT programmes; visiting therapists monitor, assess and plan programmes, but SENCos should keep good records of these visits.

Down's syndrome

Down's syndrome is a chromosomal abnormality resulting in some degree of developmental and general learning difficulty. Those with Down's syndrome are usually happy and sociable and grow to lead independent lives. TAs should encourage independence and reinforce learning by use of pictures, concrete materials, and simple language structures.

Language and Communication Difficulties (LCD)

Speech and language therapists in some health districts are beginning to train TAs to work with them in teaching children with some of the less severe speech and language problems, who can be supported by school-based programmes. In such cases the SENCo may be responsible for ensuring both good teamwork and record-keeping.

Autistic Spectrum Disorder (ASD)

This term describes those with a range of difficulties, usually effecting social interaction, communication and imagination. Pupils may find working with other pupils difficult. They are likely to be anxious when routines change. TAs will need to remain calm and consistent and help communication, but most of all, be aware of individual needs of those they support.

Asperger's syndrome

Thought to be a milder form of autism, but with a similar range of difficulties, pupils may be able to do well in school subject learning with support and where anxiety is controlled. But they may be unaware of classmates' feelings, and because it is typical of this group to take things literally, have difficulty understanding some aspects of what they hear and read. TAs may help by interpreting the social world and keeping the pupil calm.

Hearing Impairment (HI)

TAs employed to support those with hearing impairment may have learnt to sign where this is appropriate. They will work closely with the visiting teachers of the deaf who will advise on suitable ways to support the child within the curriculum. Knowledge of how hearing aids give students access to the curriculum is essential, but also a realisation of their limitations. It is very important to recognise that those with a HI cannot listen to the teacher and the TA simultaneously, making in-class support problematical.

Visual Impairment (VI)

TAs employed to support pupils who have significant levels of VI often carry out specific tasks such as being responsible for enlarging worksheets. This requires advice from a visiting teacher for VI who liaises with subject or class teachers. Some pupils will need to learn Braille, others will benefit from learning to type. TAs sometimes have special training to act as instructors for these skills.

Specific Learning Difficulties (SpLD): dyspraxia

This is a specific learning difficulty which effects movement. It may result in poor performance in sport and clumsiness in other activities. It is likely to affect handwriting, making the process slow and results unsatisfactory. TAs may need to help with planning, organising and social interaction. Advice should be available from an Occupational Therapist.

Specific Learning Difficulties (SpLD): dyslexia

Definitions vary, but one of the core difficulties is a problem with acquisition of literacy skills; reading, spelling and writing. This is often compounded by frustration and poor self-image. Those with SpLD often have poor organisational skills, forget instructions and lose their belongings. TAs can help pupils by establishing routines and quietly checking that the pupil knows these. Many of those with dyslexia are able thinkers and resent being patronised, so students views should be listened to as to how they wish to be supported.

Behavioural, Emotional and Social Difficulties (BESD)

The group of pupils with emotional or behavioural difficulties presents a different kind of challenge. Clearly they too need access to the curriculum and help to overcome blocks to learning which arise from their internal state of anxiety or fear of risk-taking. Teachers too need a different quality of support when facing challenging or worrying behaviour, establishing classroom rules and building positive relationships. A behaviour policy for the school should not only be about rules, rewards and sanctions, but cover staff development and the support needs of teachers. Learning mentors appointed for those pupils at risk of exclusion, may sometimes replace the use of a TA for those with BESD. TAs who have received training, may also be part of an LA support service (BEST).

Attention Deficit Disorder (ADD/ADHD)

This term is used to describe the condition of children with long-term difficulties in attention, hyperactivity and impulsive behaviour. Such children can be distracting and irritating to classmates and teachers. Much of what has been said about BESD will apply, but recognition needs to be given that because of the condition, the child's behaviour is not fully under their control. The definition is a medical one, and may result in the prescription of medication. (See Source List 1b for further reading on all of the above.)

Appendix 9: Statement of Special Educational Needs: Appendices

A: parental advice
B: educational advice (usually from the school but specialist teachers advice may be added where applicable)
C: medical advice (doctors and therapists)
D: psychological advice
E: advice from the Social Services Authority (this is not completed if the child is not known to Social Services)
F: other advice obtained by the authority
G: advice obtained by the authority since the last assessment of the child under section 323 of the Education Act 1996 was made.

(See Code of Practice (2001) Schedule 2, Regulation 16, p. 43.)

Appendix 10a: Different ways of observing children

Observation is a way of finding out more, but first it is necessary to ask – Why observe?

Why observe?

Answers could be:

- as a means of generating hypotheses.
- as a means of answering specific questions; how often does a child do that?
- as a way to better understand children and their viewpoints and behaviours.

This last point is the most relevant to those wishing to learn about pupil perspectives.

Next ask: what should we observe?

This could be a matter of choosing the scale of the focus, either:

- large units of activity, e.g. playground behaviour, or
- specific activities, e.g. reading strategies, or
- facial expressions, gestures, eye movements within specific contexts.

Next ask: how should the observations be done?

They could be in the form of:

- *Diaries*: biographies over time, e.g. day, week;
- *Single episode recording*;
- *Time sampling*: e.g. 1 minute every 15 minutes;
- *Event sampling*: record specific type of event wherever it happens;
- *Tracking*: observing child in different contexts or with different adults over a fixed period.

What form will recording take?

- narrative descriptions;
- prepared checklists to tick or mark with symbols;
- audio or video tape analysis.

All have advantages and some suit certain techniques best. Narrative is necessary for diaries, tracking and events sampling. Checklists are best for time sampling. A mixture of methods may produce the best all-round picture.

Cautions

- All observations take time – analysis can be even more time consuming.
- Focus as much as possible; be selective but be aware of bias from this selection.
- Note what you see; not your inferences, draw no conclusions without evidence.
- Be aware of observer bias – two observers may produce a clearer picture of reality.
- Try to see things from the pupil's perspective, not yours.
- Prepare carefully to avoid missing things because you cannot record quickly or accurately enough.
- Warn colleagues of your activities and do not underestimate pupils. They might ask 'What are you doing?' if your behaviour is too peculiar!
- What part will spoken language play? Will this be recorded with the observation and if so, how?
- How valid are your observations? Can you check these with the child?

Examples

Time sampling

Advantages

- useful when behaviours to be observed are frequent;
- or, when behaviours are distinct and early recognised;

- it takes less time if prepared well;
- provides quantifiable data;
- useful for baseline information.

Disadvantages

- doesn't tell much about pupil perspectives;
- omits context and interaction between behaviours;
- can distort reality because cause and effect may not be noted.

Event sampling

- useful to learn more about a selective type of behaviour in detail;
- or when a whole event can be recorded and analysed;
- where context – antecedents and consequences can be noted – good for the ABC analysis of behaviour;
- can be used for infrequent events;
- pupil views can be included.

Disadvantages

- more difficult to prepare for thoroughly;
- needs more analysis after the observation.

Tracking

- useful for finding out the effect of different teachers and different experiences on a child to find out reasons for a problem.

Disadvantages

- taking the time to do this may be difficult;
- colleagues need to agree and understand purposes;
- being inconspicuous may be difficult; the observer may make pupil behaviours different;
- focus on one pupil might be difficult to disguise and could cause embarrassment;
- observer's activity must be plausible to the peer group.

The best way may be to use a mixture of techniques and data and to balance one with another. *Remember*: observation material is confidential and must be used to provide information to solve a problem or gain useful information *to help the child or children*. Once used it should not be kept in any way that could identify the pupil. Pupils and parents have rights. Ask permission of parents, if at all possible. Observation will provide data, set up hypotheses and is one source of information, but pupils' views will need to be collected as well as the views of parents and other professionals to check out its validity.

Appendix 10b: Example of questionnaire for primary pupils	Use the faces to find out how children feel about your area of enquiry. Ask your questions orally and use the first two to get the group used to the idea of colouring in or ticking the face that is most like 'how they feel when . . .' for example, watching your favourite TV programme. Then ask about 'how they feel when . . .' asking the research questions. (Used by the ILEA Research for eight-year-olds looking into pupils' views about learning to read and write from ILEA Research and Statistics 1988.)

1

2

3

4

Appendix 10c: Definition of a parent (from glossary of Code and the Children Act 1989)

A parent includes any person:

- who is not a natural parent of the child but who has parental responsibility for him or her, or
- who has care of the child.

Parental responsibility under section 2 of the Children Act falls upon:

- all mothers and fathers who were married to each other at the time of the child's birth;
- mothers who were not married to the father at the time of the child's birth;
- fathers who were not married to the mother at the time of the child's birth, but who have parental responsibility either by agreement with the child's mother or through a court order.

References

Adey, P. and Shayer, M. (1994) *Really Raising Standards: Cognitive intervention and academic achievement*. London: Routledge.

Allan, J. (1999) *Actively Seeking Inclusion: Pupils with special needs in mainstream schools*. London: Falmer Press.

Allan, J. (2003) 'Productive pedagogies and the challenge of inclusion', *British Journal of Special Education*, 30(4), 175–9.

Aspect (2005) *School Self-evaluation: A process of change*. www.aspect.org.uk

Audit Commission/HMI (1992) *Getting the Act Together – Provision for pupils with special educational needs: A management handbook for schools and local education authorities*. London: HMSO.

Balshaw, M. H. (1999) *Help in the Classroom*, 2nd edn. London: David Fulton Publishers.

Barton, L. (1997) 'Inclusive education: romantic, subversive or realistic?', *International Journal of Inclusive Education*, 1(3), 235–48.

Black, P. and Wiliam, D. (1998) *Inside the Black Box: Raising standards through classroom assessment*. London: Kings College.

Blagg, N., Ballinger, M. and Gardner, R. (1988) *Somerset Thinking Skills*. Oxford: Basil Blackwell and Somerset County Council.

Brandon, M., Howe, A., Dagley, V., Salter, C., Warren, C. and Black, J. (2006) *Evaluating the Common Assessment Framework and Lead Professional Guidance and Implementation in 2005–6*. Brief no. RB740. Nottingham: DfES.

Bruner, J. (1968) *Towards a Theory of Instruction*. New York: W. W. Norton.

Buck, D. and Davis, V. (2001) *Assessing Pupils' Performance Using the P Scales*. London: David Fulton Publishers.

Cheminais, R. (2005) *Every Child Matters: A new role for SENCos*. London: David Fulton Publishers.

Clarke, S. (2001) *Unlocking Formative Assessment: Practical strategies for enhancing pupils' learning in the primary classroom*. London: Hodder and Stoughton.

Claxton, G. (2005) 'Each to their own', *Education Guardian*, 31 May.

Cleese, A., Daniels, H. and Norwich, B (1997) *Teacher Support Teams in Primary and Secondary Schools*. London: David Fulton Publishers.

Croll, P. and Moses, D. (2000) *Special Needs in the Primary School*. London: Cassell.

Cowne, E. A. (1993) 'Conversational uses of the Repertory Grid for personal learning and the management of change in Special Educational Needs', unpublished Ph.D. thesis, Uxbridge: Brunel University.

Cowne, E. A. (2003) *Developing Inclusive Practice: The SENCo's role in managing change*. London: David Fulton Publishers.

Cowne, E. A. and Murphy, M. (2000) *A Beginner's Guide to SEN: A handbook*. Tamworth: NASEN.

Cowne, E. A. and Robertson, C. (2005) 'Editorial', *Support for Learning*, 20(2), 51.

Dale, N. (1996) *Working with Families with Special Needs: Partnership and practice*. London: Routledge.

Dearing, R. (1994) *The National Curriculum and its Assessment*. London: SCAA.

DCSF (2006) The Childcare Act. Norwich: The Stationery Office.

DCSF (2007a) *The Standards Website*, www.standards.dcsf.gov.uk/secondary/keystage3

DCSF (2007b) *Statutory Guidance in DCSF (2007) Statutory Framework*. Nottingham: DCSF.

DCSF (2007c) *The Use of Performance Scales for Children with Special Educational Needs*, dcsf.gsi.gov.uk.

DES (1944) *Education Act*. London: HMSO.

DES (1959) *Handicapped Pupils and Special Educational Needs Regulations*. London: HMSO.

DES (1970) *Handicapped Children Act*. London: HMSO.

DES (1978) *Special Educational Needs: Report of the committee of enquiry into the education of handicapped children and young people* (The Warnock report). London: HMSO.

DES (1981) Education Act. London: HMSO.

DES (1983, 1984, 1985) *The In-service Training Grants Scheme*, Circulars 3/83, 4/84, 5/85. London: HMSO.

DES (1988) Education Reform Act. London: HMSO.

DfE (1993) The Education Act. London: HMSO.

DfE (1994) *The Code of Practice on the Identification and Assessment of Special Educational Needs*. London: HMSO.

DfEE (1996) The Education Act. London: HMSO.

DfEE (1998) *Programme for Action*. London: HMSO.

DfEE (1999) *Social Inclusion: Pupil Support*. Circular 10/99.

DfEE and QCA (1999a) *The National Curriculum Handbook for Primary Teachers in England*, 'Inclusion statement', p. 30. London: DfEE.

DfEE and QCA (1999b) *The National Curriculum Handbook for Secondary Teachers in England*, 'Inclusion statement', p. 32. London: DfEE.

DfES (2001a) Special Educational Needs Disability Act (SENDA). London: The Stationery Office.

DfES (2001b) *Special Educational Needs Code of Practice*, no. 581. London: DfES.

DfES (2001c) *SEN Toolkit*, no.558. London: DfES.

DfES (2003) *Excellence and Enjoyment: A strategy for primary schools*. London: DfES. 0518 2004.

DfES (2004a) *Every Child Matters: Change for children in schools*. London: DfES.

DfES (2004b) The Children Act. Norwich: HMSO.

DfES (2004c) *Removing Barriers to Achievement: The government's strategy for SEN*. Nottingham: DfES.

DfES (2004d) *Introductory Training for School Support Staff: Risk and reflection*. London: DfES 0607.

DfES (2005) *Leading on Inclusion*. London: DfES 1183–2005G, www.standards.dfes.gov.uk/primary/publications/inclusion

DfES (2006a) The Education and Inspections Act. London: DfES.

DfES (2006b) *Implementing the Disability Discrimination Act in Schools and Early Years Settings*. London: DfES.

DfES (2007a) *Personalised Learning*, www.standards.dfes.gov.uk/personalisedlearning/about

DfES (2007b) *Statutory Framework for the Early Years Foundation Stage*. Nottingham: DfES.

DfES/DoH (2002) *Guidance on the Use of Physical Interventions for Staff Working with Children and Adults Who Display Extreme Behaviour*. LEA.0242/2002.

Disability Rights Commission (DRC) (1995) Disability Discrimination Act. London: HMSO.

DRC (2002a) *Code of Practice for Post 16*. London: The Stationery Office.

DRC (2002b) *Code of Practice for Schools*. London: The Stationery Office.

DHSS (1989) The Children Act. London: HMSO.

Donaldson, M. (1978) *Children's Minds*. Glasgow: Fontana.

DRC (2005) The Disability Discrimination Act.

Evans, J., Everard, B., Friend, J., Glazer, A., Norwich, B. and Welton, J. (1981) *Decision-making for Special Educational Needs: An inter-service resource pack*. London: University of London, Institute of Education.

FEFC (1996) *Inclusive Learning: The Report of the Learning Difficulties/and or Disabilities Committee* (The Tomlinson Report). Coventry: Further Education Funding Council.

Feuerstein, R., Rand, Y., Hoffman, M. and Miller, M. (1980) *Instrumental Enrichment: An intervention programme for cognitive modifiability*. Baltimore, MD: University Park Press.

Fish, J. (1989) *What Is Special Education?* Milton Keynes: Open University Press.

Florian, L. (1998) 'Inclusive practice', in Tilstone, C. Florian, L., and Rose, R., *Promoting Inclusive Practice*. London: Routledge.

Fox, G. (2003) *A Handbook for Learning Support Assistants: Teachers and assistants working together*. London: David Fulton Publishers.

Fullan, M. (2003) *Change Forces with a Vengeance*. London: Falmer Press.

Galloway, D. (1985) *Schools, Pupils and Special Educational Needs*. London: Croom Helm.

Gardner, H. (1983) *Frames of Mind: The theory of multiple intelligence*. New York: Basic Books.

Gascoigne, E. (1995) *Working with Parents as Partners in SEN*. London: David Fulton Publishers.

Gerschel, L. (2005) 'The special educational needs coordinator's role in managing teaching assistants: the Greenwich experience', *Support for Learning*, 20(2), 69–76.

Gipps, C. (1992) *What We Know about Effective Primary Teaching*. London: Institute of Education and Tufnell Press.

Gross, J. and White, A. (2003) *Special Educational Needs and School Improvement: Practical strategies for raising standards*. London: David Fulton Publishers.

Hall, D. (2001) *Assessing the Needs of Bilingual Pupils*, 2nd edn. London: David Fulton Publishers.

Hanko, G. (1995) *Special Needs in Ordinary Classrooms: From staff support to staff development* 3rd edn. London: David Fulton Publishers.

Hanko, G. (2003) 'Towards an inclusive school culture – but what happened to Elton's "affective curriculum"', *British Journal of Special Education*, 30(3), 125–30.

Hargreaves, D., Deforges, C., Goswani, U. and Wood, D. (2005) *Report of the Learning Working Group*. Demos, www.demos.co.uk

Hart, S. (1991) 'The collaborative classroom', in McLaughlin, C. and Rouse, M. (eds), *Supporting Schools*. London: David Fulton Publishers.

Hart, S. (1995) 'Down a different path', Discussion Paper 1, 33–42. *Schools' SEN Policy Pack*. London: National Childrens Bureau.

Holley, G. (2007) 'Extended schools', *Education Guardian*, 25 September.

Hornby, G. (2001) 'Promoting responsible inclusion: quality education for all', in O'Brien, T (ed.), *Enabling Inclusion: Blue skies . . . dark clouds?* London: The Stationery Office.

House of Commons Education and Skills Committee (2006) *Special Educational Needs*, Vol.1. Ref: HC478-1. London: The Stationery Office.

Hrekow, M. (2006) *Provision Management for Inclusion: Guidance materials.* London: Special Educational Needs Joint Initiative for Training (SENJIT).

Implementation Review Statement on SEN and disability (2007) www.teachernet. gov.uk/wholeschool/sen

Inhelder, B. and Piaget, J. (1958) *The Growth of Logical Thinking.* London: Routledge and Kegan Paul.

Layton, L. (2005) 'Special Educational Needs coordinators and leadership: a role too far?', *Support for Learning*, 20(2), 53–60.

Lewis, A., Parsons, S. and Robertson, C. (2006) *My school, my family, my life: Telling it like it is.* Disability Rights Commission.

LSC (2004) *LSC School Support Staff Sector Plan for 2004–5 and Beyond.* London: Learning and Skills Council.

Lorenz, S. (1998) *Effective In-class Support.* London: David Fulton Publishers.

MacConville, R., Dedridge, S., Gyulai, A., Palmer, J. and Rhys-Davies, L. (2007) *Looking at Inclusion: Listening to the voices of young people.* London: Paul Chapman.

MacGilchrist, B. and Buttress, M. (2005) *Transforming Learning and Teaching.* London: Paul Chapman.

Montgomery, D. (2003) *Gifted and Talented Children with Special Educational Needs: Double exceptionality.* London: NACE/Fulton.

Mosley, J. (1993) *Turn Your School Round.* Wisbech: Learning Development Aids (LDA).

NCB/SENJIT (2005) *Schools SEN Policy Pack*, Unit B. London: National Childrens Bureau.

National Curriculum Council (NCC) (1989) *Implementing the National Curriculum: Participation by pupils with SEN*, Circular No. 5. York: NCC.

Newton, C. and Wilson, D. (1999) *Circles of Friends.* Dunstable: Folens.

Norwich, B. (1990a) *Reappraising Special Education.* London: Cassell.

Norwich, B. (1990b) 'How entitlement can become a restraint', in Daniels, H. and Ware, J. (eds), *Special Educational Needs and the National Curriculum.* London: Kogan Page and University of London, Institute of Education.

NUT (2004) *Special Educational Needs Coordinators and the Revised Code of Practice: An NUT survey.* London: National Union of Teachers.

O'Brien, T. (2001) 'Learning from the hard cases', in O'Brien, T. (ed.), *Enabling Inclusion: Blue skies . . . dark clouds?* London: The Stationery Office.

O'Brien, T. and Guiney, D. (2001) *Differentiation in Teaching and Learning, Principles and Practice.* London: Continuum.

Ofsted (1996) *Promoting High Achievement for Pupils with SEN.* London: HMSO.

Ofsted (2005) *Inclusion: The impact of LEA support and outreach services.* London: HMI 2452.

Ofsted (2006) *Inclusion: Does it matter where pupils are taught?* London: HMSO.

O'Hanlon, C. (1993) 'Changing the school by reflectively re-defining the role of the special needs coordinator', in Dyson, A. and Gains, C. (eds), *Rethinking Special Needs in Mainstream Schools towards the Year 2000*, pp. 99–109. London: David Fulton Publishers.

QCA (1999b) *The Revised National Curriculum.* London: QCA.

QCA/DfEE (2000) *Curriculum Guidance for the Foundation Stage.* London: DfEE.

Robertson, C. (1999) 'Initial teacher education and inclusive schooling', *Support for Learning*, 14(4), 169–73.

Robertson, C. (2001) 'The social model of disability and the rough ground of inclusive education', in O'Brien, T. (ed.), *Enabling Inclusion: Blue skies . . . dark clouds?* London: The Stationery Office.

Sebba, J., Brown, N., Steward, S., Galton, M. and James, M., with Celento, N. and

Boddy, P. (2007) *An Investigation of Personalised Learning: Approaches used by schools*. London: DfES.

Skinner, B. F. (1974) *About Behaviourism*. London: Jonathan Cape.

Sproson, B. (2003) 'Solution or smoke screen: the use of further education colleges in making KS4 provision for difficult to manage (D2M) students, *Support for Learning*, 18(1), 18–23.

Stationery Office, The (TSO) (2002) *Code of Practice for Schools: Disability Discrimination Act 1995: Part 4*. London: The Stationery Office.

Stationery Office, The (TSO) (2005) *The Duty to Promote Disability Equality: Statutory Code of Practice*. London: The Stationery Office.

Sutton, A. (1982) 'The Powers that be', Unit 8, E241 course material. Milton Keynes: Open University Press.

Teacher Development Agency (TDA) (2006) *Teaching Assistant File*. London: Teacher Development Agency.

Teacher Training Agency (TTA) (1998) *National Standards for Special Educational Needs Coordinators*. London: Teacher Training Agency.

Tizard, B. and Hughes, M. (1984) *Young Children Learning*. Glasgow: Fontana.

Tomlinson, S. (1982) *A Sociology of Special Education*. London: Routledge and Kegan Paul.

Tutt, R. (2007a) *Every Child Included*. London: Paul Chapman

Tutt, R. (2007b) 'Beyond the Inclusion Debate' *Special Children March–April*, 32–7.

Vygotsky, L. S. (1978) *Mind in Society*. Cambridge, MA: Harvard University Press.

Warnock, M. (2005) *Special Educational Needs: A new look*. London: Philosophy of Education Society of Great Britain.

Wedell, K. (1980) 'Early identification and compensatory interaction', in Knights, R. M. and Bakker, D. J. (eds), *Treatment of Hyperactive and Learning Disordered Children*. Baltimore, MD: University Park Press.

Wedell, K. (2005) 'The Gulliford lecture: dilemmas in the quest for inclusion', *British Journal of Special Education*, 32(1), 3–11.

Wedell, K. (2006) 'Points from the SENCo-Forum', *British Journal of Special Education*, 33(2), 98.

Weller, K. and Craft, A. (1983) *Making Up Our Minds: An exploratory study of instrumental enrichment*. London: Schools Council Publications.

Wragg, E. C. (1997) *The Cubic Curriculum*. London: Routledge.

Index